D1616899

AN AUTO/BIOGRAPHICAL APPROACH TO LEARNING DISABILITY RESEARCH

For Bert, Bill, George, Edna
Margaret, Albert, John, Denzil and Brian

An Auto/Biographical Approach to Learning Disability Research

DOROTHY ATKINSON
School of Health and Social Welfare
The Open University
Walton Hall
Milton Keynes

Ashgate

Aldershot • Brookfield USA • Singapore • Sydney

© Dorothy Atkinson 1997

Published by
Ashgate Publishing Ltd
Gower House
Croft Road
Aldershot
Hants GU11 3HR
England

Ashgate Publishing Company
Old Post Road
Brookfield
Vermont 05036
USA

British Library Cataloguing in Publication Data

Atkinson, Dorothy, 1945-
    An auto/biographical approach to learning disability
    research
    1. Learning disabilities - Research 2. Learning disabled -
    Biography
    I. Title
    371.9

Library of Congress Catalog Card Number: 97-72080

ISBN 1 85628 645 2

Printed and bound by Athenaeum Press, Ltd.,
Gateshead, Tyne & Wear.

Contents

Acknowledgements

The preparation of this book has taken place over several stages, including the work involved in the research project which forms the very heart of the story. I wish to thank the many organizations, groups and individuals who have contributed in various ways, and at various stages, in the planning and execution of the research, and in the subsequent preparation and writing of this book.

The research would not have been possible without the support and encouragement of the Open University's School of Health and Social Welfare and Bedfordshire Social Services Department. Thanks are due, respectively, to Malcolm Johnson and Gill Brown for their help in getting the research off the ground. The project depended for its success on the goodwill and unstinting enthusiasm of Mo Bates, Janet Brown and Ann Lorman who, at the time, were key staff at the residential home and day centre. My warmest thanks are due to them for helping to keep the project going through organizing transport, offering reassurance, joining in with their own memories, and helping to interpret group members' responses.

The project was a success because of the nine people who volunteered to join the history group, and who stayed with it for its two-year lifetime. Very special thanks are due to Bert Angell, Bill Baker, George Coley, Edna Day, Margaret Day, Albert Gaylor, John Rivers, Denzil Smith and Brian Sutcliffe for joining the group and contributing so much to the project and, ultimately, to this book. I am indebted, for my own greater understanding and awareness of how life used to be, to the nine members of the group.

Thanks are due also to the people who supported me throughout the research. In this context I want to thank Ann Brechin and Jan Walmsley for their initial help in devising themes; to Joanna Bornat for her advice on how to do oral history; and to Fiona Williams for sharing ideas on life story work and identity. I am grateful to the members of the Reflective Research Group for listening to my uncertainties and for suggesting how I might deal with them.

The project led to the publication *Past Times*. Thanks are due to Christine Finch for her work in typing the various drafts, and for devising just the right format for the final version. I also want to thank Wendy Lee for facilitating the private publication of *Past Times*, and for proof reading the present book.

Several other people have been involved in the preparation and writing of this book, and I want to thank them personally. Many thanks are due to Janet Vango for her excellent typing of various drafts, her patient attention to detail and for her untiring commitment to making history accessible in book form. I also want to thank Ann Brechin, Joanna Bornat, Di Harden and Mark Jackson for taking the time to read the manuscript in draft, and for giving me the encouragement and feedback I needed to revise and improve it. Special thanks are due to Jan Walmsley not only for reading the book, but also for sharing many ideas, conversations and conference papers along the way. My final thanks are to Peter Sharpe for his personal support of the project and for always being there when there were deadlines to be met and time was short.

1 Introduction

The silence of centuries

Many things have been claimed on behalf of people with learning disabilities. One claim is that their voices have been 'lost' not just across the years of this century, but throughout all time. There is a sense in which theirs are the 'ultimate lost voices' in terms of autobiographical records (Atkinson and Walmsley, 1995). With little or no recourse to the written word, their voices were seldom if ever heard. Certainly there is, and has been, silence on the part of people with learning disabilities, a silence throughout the centuries.

The silence is pervasive. One consequence is that much lived history, in the form of the personal experiences of people with learning disabilities, has gone unrecorded. There are few individual accounts of people's lives, and hardly any sense of a shared perspective on history. The history (or histories) of people with learning disabilities, from their point of view, remains largely unwritten. In that sense it is a hidden history. It is hidden not only from the people most centrally concerned but hidden from all of us.

The silence has been filled, of course, by other more influential and powerful voices. As Joanna Ryan observed, 'What history they do have is not so much theirs as the history of others acting on their behalf or against them' (1980, p. 85). Thus there *is* a history of sorts; a partial account, based on documented evidence. This is a history of landmarks, key events, Acts of Parliament, and the deeds of great men (and, in this case, of women). These accounts do not include the views of people whose lives were touched, changed or even shaped by the events and actions which feature in these formal accounts. These accounts are not, of course, accessible to people with learning disabilities. The formal history of learning disability, just as much as the lived histories of real people, remains hidden from those most centrally concerned.

1

This book looks at ways and means of recovering (or finding) at least some of those lost voices, and beginning to chart aspects of that hidden history. In so doing, it is hoped that people who are still largely 'invisible' in their local communities (Bornat, 1992) will become visible and known. This is where what I am calling auto/biographical research comes in. This is a convenient umbrella term which includes both biographical research, which seeks to draw out and compile individual biographies or life stories, and oral history, which involves individuals and groups in recounting their lives within an historical context.

Auto/biographical research can have an impact at both a personal and a social level. At a personal level, it provides the opportunity for people with learning disabilities to look at, and make sense of, their own lives. In enabling people to compile their autobiographies it involves them in the process of life review.

At a social level, the collecting of auto/biographical accounts can bring out the commonalities as well as the differences in people's experiences – commonalities with other people with learning disabilities, as well as with the rest of society. This has the potential to encourage social and historical awareness, and understanding, of shared experiences, and their sources, for people with learning disabilities. And, just as importantly, auto/biographical research provides a means by which the understanding of others can be enriched – so we can begin to know what it means, and what it has meant, to be seen as a person with a learning disability in this society.

Revealing hidden history – or histories

People with learning disabilities have been silent, or perhaps it is more accurate to say *silenced,* for much of the century. They do speak now and, to an ever increasing degree, they are heard. But this is a late twentieth century phenomenon. They were until recently silent and, in their silence, other people spoke about them and spoke for – or against – them.

In the early years of this century people with learning disabilities were seen as a threat to society. This meant they were segregated from everyone else and were literally out of earshot. They were effectively silenced. As 'deficit' theories came into vogue, first in medicine and psychology, but later in education, then people were seen as cases to be treated (or specially trained). The voices of people themselves were replaced by their case histories, prepared by others on their behalf. As social theories came into fashion from the 1960s and 70s onwards, people with learning disabilities were represented not as the perpetrators of social ills but more the victims of social oppression. Now at the end of the century their own voices are increasingly being heard. Neither 'villains' nor 'victims', in their own accounts they are individuals with a personal history, a culture, a class, a gender, as well as an impairment (Atkinson and Williams, 1990, p. 8).

The silence, then, was never total. Voices have been heard throughout the century, but mostly these were not the voices of people with learning disabilities. Whose voices were they? And what were they saying? I will look, in turn, at the voices heard most clearly in the four key phases in the history of learning disability in this century: the phases of segregation, experts, normalization and self-advocacy.

1 Silence through segregation

At the turn of the century, and until the 1930s, many of the voices were those of the eugenicists, and those sympathetic to their cause. A link had been made, or at least claimed, between 'mental deficiency' (as it was then known) and all kinds of social problems. In 1896, the National Association for the Care and Control of the Feeble-Minded was set up, a pressure group which campaigned for the lifelong segregation of 'mental defectives' (the terminology of the time). Its aim was to prevent sexuality, and thus the reproduction of mental defectives – echoing, according to Joanna Ryan, wider middle class fears at the time regarding working class fertility (1980, p. 107).

Underlying the campaign was the belief that mental defectives were not only the cause of most social evils but were also an economic burden (Fido and Potts 1989). The National Association and the Eugenics Society joined forces in 1910 in order to campaign for mental deficiency legislation. Jointly the two organizations issued a pamphlet pressing for urgent action:

> [...] BECAUSE in consequence of the neglect to recognize and treat their condition, the mentally defective become criminals and are sent to prison; they become drunkards and fill the reformatories; they become paupers, and pass into the workhouses.

> BECAUSE they are frequently producing children, many of whom inherit their mental defect, and nearly all of whom become the paupers, criminals and unemployables of the next generation.

Fiona Williams (1993) sees this view of learning disability as a first attempt to place it within a wider social context. This analysis saw mental defectives essentially as the villains of the piece. The present bid to place learning disability within a wider social context has changed the emphasis – in current thinking the erstwhile villains have become the victims of oppression. But we shall come to this view later.

The ideas of the eugenics movement were influential at the turn of the century. These ideas dominated how people with learning disabilities were seen both as a social group and as individuals representative of that social group. Mental deficiency in this context was seen as a social problem associated with race degeneration and threatened deterioration of the national stock.

The 1913 Mental Deficiency Act established the basis of a separate and unified service which was intended to exclude mentally deficient people from other welfare and social agencies, and to bar them from the general educational system. This was the beginning of the policies of exclusion which have operated, one way and another, for much of this century. An energetic nationwide crusade for most, if not all, mental defectives to be institutionalized for life – 'for their protection and the protection of others' – had been influential in the passing of the Act. As a result, the Act required local authorities to certify all mental defectives and set up special certified institutions. The drive to institutionalization was based, according to Fido and Potts (1989), on the overriding fear that the feeble-minded would 'repeat their type', resulting in the 'propagation of a degenerate stock'. There was a particular concern about young feeble-minded women, as they were presumed to be more immoral and fertile than other women (Digby, 1996; Atkinson and Walmsley, 1995).

This concern found expression in the 1913 Act, which created a whole new category of 'unfit' mothers – 'feeble-minded women'. This was a socially constructed category, which led to the wholesale identification and categorization of women said to be feeble-minded. The classification feeble-minded was equated with assumed immorality, fecundity, promiscuity and disease (Williams, 1993). The 1913 Act was a means of controlling the sexual threat seen to be posed by these women, not least because they could be targeted for institutional segregation (Digby, 1996; Thomson, 1992; Atkinson and Walmsley, 1995). The incarceration of thousands of women on this basis had a lasting and profound effect on the women concerned, and their families. Some of their life stories, which include their experiences of identification and incarceration, have subsequently been recorded and published (Potts and Fido, 1991).

The first step to detainment and institutionalization was certification, involving the assessment of people according to three levels of defect: 'idiot', 'imbecile' and 'feeble-minded', together with a catch-all category of 'moral defective'. This latter category was used to detain many people, often adolescents, on account of minor offences, like petty thefts, or having an illegitimate baby.

This era generated its own set of stories. At the time, biographical accounts were used as part of the campaign preceding the Act for lifelong institutionalization. Now different sorts of life stories are emanating from this era. Some of those people who were certified, and institutionalized, under the terms of the Act are now contributing their autobiographical accounts of their admission and subsequent incarceration in long-stay institutions. The two sets of stories have little in common.

2 Experts speak

In the period 1930s–1980s the medical approach dominated the learning disability field. It did so to such an extent that Joanna Ryan suggests it provides a case study of the 'medicalization of a social problem' and is 'indicative of the way our society deals with people it finds useless, dangerous or inconvenient' (Ryan, 1980, p. 15). People come to be labelled as 'different' for all sorts of reasons. One explanation which has been dominant for much of this century is that people with learning disabilities are, on certain objective and measurable criteria, 'deficient' in cognitive and social skills (and, at times, seen as lesser beings in moral terms). The deficit model of learning disability has justified the kind of 'treatment' that people with learning disabilities have received throughout much of this century. It also helped fuel the rise and dominance of the 'expert'.

There have been many experts in learning disability in this century. Doctors, especially psychiatrists, psychologists and educationalists have all identified deficits in the people who came their way. These deficits could be treated and ameliorated by various specialist programmes such as drugs regimes, behaviour programmes, skills training and special needs teaching. The dominant voice in the treatment era was the voice of the expert. The voices of people with learning disabilities, if heard at all, were submerged into the case histories written about them. People's lives became 'biographical fragments' in the accounts of others (Walmsley, 1996).

This process reflects what Joanna Ryan has called 'medical model' thinking. This typically takes a narrow view of the people it is dealing with, seeing them in terms of what is wrong or abnormal about them, and focusing on the nature of 'the defect' (Ryan, 1980, p. 26). This view, however, is held without due regard for environmental factors, or the social context in which people were living. The view, and the explanation, were couched in terms of the shortcomings or problems of the person with learning disability. Treatment was on the basis of how to make good those shortcomings, or how to change or suppress the person's 'behaviour problems'. At the turn of the century, doctors came to see themselves as experts in mental deficiency, writing papers and books on, for example, feeble-mindedness as a physical condition (Digby, 1996; Jackson, 1996).

5

Medicine sanctioned the long-stay hospitals as places in which to treat people whom society had rejected. Patients were seen in pathological terms; admission and 'care' were deemed necessary on the basis of what was diagnosed as wrong with them. This process had both personal and social consequences. At a personal level, this approach masked or denied other aspects of people's existence. At a social level, it continued and expanded the policy of exclusion of people with learning disabilities for much of this century.

There were flaws in the defect theories themselves. In stressing the pathological explanation of learning disability, the defect theories led to a medical approach which assessed and measured the differences between people with learning disabilities and 'normal' people. They focused on, for example, their slow reaction time, their inconsistent learning strategies, and their inadequate short-term memories (Ryan, 1980, p. 27). The defect theories emphasized how people were different and inferior; they did not look for commonalities between people (a point made by Bogdan and Taylor, 1982). Implicit in the terminology of mental deficiency was the notion of the mental defective as 'the Other' (Digby, 1996). And the scientific discourse of the time held that mental defectives were genetically different from the rest of 'us' (Barker, 1989).

This focus on difference had a dual effect. Not only did it deny any possibility that people with learning disabilities might have a valid perception of their own situation – and be able to articulate it – but it also served to protect the rest of us from having to confront their pain and act on it. Writing in 1980, before the current interest in oral history and auto/biographical research, Joanna Ryan suggested the need 'to try and capture their experience of the world' – only then, she concluded, would we reach those 'points of identification [those] needs they share with others' (1980, p. 27).

Medical domination began to give way to other forces and influences, particularly in the 1970s. Educational ideas about 'special needs' became important, especially in the wake of the 1971 Education Act which declared all children educable. A host of ideas followed on, although much educational provision was in segregated special schools. Educational ideas were introduced into an adult context too, with reports supporting Social and Educational Centres to replace the traditional Adult Training Centres. Education was, of course, a socially acceptable form of intervention – although many people now challenge the separatist nature of much of the provision.

Psychologists have also been influential in assessing and training people, to make up for their deficits or to improve their behaviour. As in medicine and education, psychology drew on classification techniques, measurement, aetiology and the treatment of 'cases' (Williams, 1993). The development of skills or the suppression of anti-social behaviour were their main targets.

The period of the experts was dominated by medicine, 'special needs' and psychology. The documentation of case histories, or case studies, according to Fiona Williams (1993) became all important. One source of stories is thus the medical (or educational or psychological) case history, the biographical account written by the professional at the time. Set against the medical case history are other sets of stories which have emerged only in recent years. The oral history accounts collected and compiled by Potts and Fido (1991) provide a rare and rich insight into daily life and deprivation in a colony in the north of England. And it is my hope that this book will provide another source of auto/biographical accounts to set alongside and against the case histories of the experts.

3   The 'villain' becomes the 'victim'

The shift in perspective whereby the 'villain' of the early twentieth century came to be seen, in the later years of the century, as its 'victim', can be traced back to a set of sociological theories which came into prominence in the 1960s. These were the theories which sought to explain deviance, stigma and devaluation, and they were used to shed new light on how people with learning disabilities had been treated for much of this century.

The learning disability 'problem' was re-cast as being not so much in the person as in the social processes which placed that person in a 'defective' role in society. Thus learning disability came to be seen by some people as socially constructed. The focus, in this school of thought, switched from the diagnosed personal deficits to the very process which had categorized and labelled the person as 'deficient' in the first place. Labelling was seen to have its own consequences, not least that a label such as 'mental defective' could all too readily become all-encompassing. It becomes (or threatens to become) the identity of the person concerned. Other personal and social consequences were said to follow the labelling process. At a personal level, there was a stigma attached (Goffman, 1963; Khan, 1985), and at least the possibility of humiliation, segregation and discrimination (Khan, 1985, p. 60).

The label, whatever it was (and labels change over the years: 'mental defective', 'subnormal', 'mentally handicapped'), carried with it a set of assumptions about the person concerned, based on stereotypical thinking about people with learning disabilities as a social group. On this basis, not only were people seen to be of low intelligence, but additional imperfections were attributed to them, such as incompetence, irrationality, unpredictability and dangerousness. In particular, people with learning disabilities were seen as unable to express their thoughts and ideas, and unable to analyse their

7

lives and current situations (Bogdan and Taylor, 1982). Their silence was assured. Clearly they had nothing of value to say. This view has, of course, been challenged subsequently but it was a partial yet pervasive view of people with learning disabilities which held sway for many years.

A useful contribution to this debate was Wolfensberger's identification of eight social roles in which people with learning disabilities were – and indeed are – cast by others (1972). In his view, people with learning disabilities have been seen as sub-human, a menace to society, as objects of dread or of pity, as holy innocents, as sick, as objects of ridicule or as eternal children. These roles are all damaging to their incumbents. The damage is caused through a process of *devaluation*, according to Paul Williams (1985). At a personal level, people with learning disabilities experience what Williams calls 'unpleasant or handicapping experiences', such as rejection by their families, segregated services and a lifetime of instability and insecurity, wasted time and opportunities, and few relationships with 'valued' others. This was seen to be a 'career of devaluation' where people with learning disabilities were seen as victims, and 'marked' in devaluing ways as different from everybody else. The damage was seen to extend beyond individual lives. People with learning disabilities constituted a marginalized group and, as a result, were seen and treated in stereotypical ways.

This was a gloomy view. But there was a way out of the spiral of devaluation, and this was through *normalization* – the opportunity for people with learning disabilities to lead ordinary lives alongside everyone else in society. The approach, philosophy or principle of normalization emerged in Scandinavia in the late 1960s, with Bengt Nirje (1969) one of it earliest proponents. Its most influential exponent was, however, Wolfensberger (1972, 1980, 1983) who developed and refined the ideas over the years. In his view, the only way to reverse the process of devaluation was through the systematic re-valuing of people. And this was where the 'human services' came in. It was their duty, on his model, to create valued social roles, and promote positive social imagery. It was argued that people with learning disabilities would come to be seen in a positive light through their association with valued others, and through taking part in ordinary everyday life in the community.

The normalization approach has been hugely influential in professional circles. It has a very practical arm via its PASS and PASSING evaluative tools and workshops, which aim to 'rate' services on their performance in creating integrated community-based lifestyles for people with learning disabilities. Normalization is, however, a professional approach, and it is another way of seeing people essentially as victims. It allows little opportunity for people themselves to counter these views. They must fit in and conform.

Other developments in parallel with normalization, and in some ways linked with the ideas, included the drive to care in the community and the bid to close down hospitals. Wolfensberger (1975), for example, developed some work on the history of maltreatment of people with learning disabilities in the USA. This reflected the important research on conditions in the long-stay hospitals which was conducted by Pauline Morris in the UK (1969). Hospitals epitomized the way in which services systematically stigmatized and devalued people with learning disabilities. Their closure came to be seen as a major step in reversing the cycle. The anti-hospital drive was taken up in this country, particularly by CMH (then called the Campaign for People with Mental Handicaps, now called Values into Action or VIA), a campaign supported by research, publications and participative workshops. In a sense, CMH pioneered the 'speaking up' process in a series of events in the 1970s in which people with learning disabilities were able to speak of their experiences. People's autobiographical experiences – often of segregated lives in hospitals – for the first time became centre stage.

Associated with the running down and closure of hospitals was the development of community-based services as an alternative. A steady stream of policy and practice documents emerged, particularly from the King's Fund Centre and CMH, on strategies for developing 'ordinary lives' for people with learning disabilities. At the same time, researchers began looking at what life in the community was actually like. Many of these studies were influenced by, or closely linked with, the prevailing ideas on normalization (Chappell, 1992). The measures used for assessing levels of community acceptance, participation and integration, and for determining the quality of life for people in residential homes, were based on how closely – or otherwise – the lives of people with learning disabilities reflected the lives of 'normal' or 'ordinary' people. Studies of social support networks, for example, were predicated on the assumed importance of contact with ordinary people (who were seen as 'valued').

This was the beginning of auto/biographical research in a more intense and systematic way. Research into the lives of people in 'ordinary' domestic dwellings presented special challenges. Not only were there ethical considerations about intrusive research techniques, but there were practical considerations about the invisibility of many aspects of everyday life. One important way of finding out about life in the community was through the lived experiences of those people out there. Auto/biographical research for the first time became seen as important and relevant. People's own accounts, of life on the inside and on the outside, have become a source of evidence about everyday life in the community, and how it compares with institutional life.

Now at the end of the century it is the turn of people with learning disabilities to speak for themselves at last. Some of the earliest opportunities came, as we saw, with the CMH participation events. The 1980s saw the formation of self-advocacy groups, People First organizations, and groups/committees in day and residential services. These developments were given a further boost with the 1990 National Health Service and Community Care Act, with its emphasis on user participation and involvement.

Self-advocacy has encouraged people to 'speak up' about their experiences; not as villains, cases, victims, burdens or joys, but as *people*, with a whole range of experiences, views and characteristics. Clearly people with learning disabilities are not an homogeneous group. Individual lives and experiences reveal differences between people in terms of their gender, class, and social and cultural background.

And yet people do have things in common too – with each other and with all of us. Bogdan and Taylor (1982) wrote passionately about that common humanity which links us all, including people with learning disabilities. In the later chapters of this book, I explore some aspects of this common humanity through people's own accounts of their lives.

One important link that people with learning disabilities share together, and which links them with people from other social groups is, of course, the labelling process by which they are seen, categorized and treated as different from 'ordinary' people. This is a social process which operates in relation to other marginalized groups too – disabled people, black people, women and mental health survivors, for example. On this basis, people with learning disabilities can be seen as an oppressed group in society – an oppressed group with links across to other oppressed groups. Thus Fiona Williams (1993) identifies 'converging stereotypes' which cut across different oppressed social groups, and suggests that not only people with learning disabilities but also black people and women, have been seen as irrational, volatile, irresponsible, excitable, childlike and with a hidden but dangerous sexuality.

One way of counteracting such stereotypes is to encourage and develop auto/biographical research. The development of people's own life stories can act very effectively as a countervailing force to the generalizations which otherwise persist. It is through their own accounts of their lives and histories that an overall history can be written about the oppression of people with learning disabilities. Written from their point of view, this collective version of a shared history, and shared histories, can help counteract the prevailing official accounts. This book will, I hope, play a part in that re-writing process.

Some life stories have already been collected (Atkinson and Williams, 1990). These testify both to the validity of individual experience (and people's different experiences based on gender, class and race) and to their shared experiences of unfairness, stigma and oppression. Fiona Williams (1993) compares the experiences which women with learning disabilities share with other women such as motherhood (and restrictions on motherhood), caring roles, sexual vulnerability, marriage, relationships and personal safety. Some of the questions raised in relation to women with learning disabilities have also, at different times, been raised in relation to the 'undeserving poor' (which have included working class, black and Irish women). Such questions include who is a 'fit' or 'unfit' mother and who, on account of assumptions made about their presumed promiscuity, vulnerability or fecundity, is to be sterilized or otherwise prohibited from parenting.

Life stories are obviously important in this context. They enable us to know about people's lives from 'the inside' (Bogdan and Taylor, 1982). The developments in self-advocacy, and in auto/biographical research, have shown that people with learning disabilities have the capacity to express themselves, and make sense of their lives, provided we are prepared to listen. The use of life stories, or biographies, gives us the potential to look at life through the eyes of people who have been labelled, and to see their world as they see and experience it. The individual life story, and the collections of various life stories, can begin to challenge the many myths which surround people with learning disabilities.

The terminology used in this book reflects terms in current use; 'learning disability' is used instead of its forerunners 'mental deficiency', 'mental subnormality' and 'mental handicap'. The term 'people with learning disabilities' replaces the designations used throughout this century: 'idiot', 'imbecile', 'feeble-minded', 'moral defective', 'subnormal', 'severely subnormal' and 'mentally handicapped'. Many of these terms have passed into ordinary language, and have become terms of abuse. The terms have supplanted each other in quite rapid succession in what Joanna Ryan suggests is 'an illusory search for a designation that is neutral or euphemistic' (Ryan, 1980, p. 11).

The search is illusory because the process of labelling itself identifies and creates social distance between people. As learning disability is usually seen negatively, so people themselves come to be viewed and treated negatively, whatever the terminology used. Ryan suggests, further, that because the labels are conceived by others, they represent the history of learning disability as seen by those others, not by people themselves. The changing definitions of difference, in Ryan's view, constitute the history of learning disability. But it is a history constructed from society's standpoint; it fails to allow people with learning disabilities to find 'their own identity, their own history' (Ryan, 1980, p. 13).

The use of auto/biographies, or life stories, is one way in which personal and social identity can be (re)-claimed and in which the history of people with learning disabilities can begin to be constructed from their point of view. Again, this book aims to play a part in that process; it looks at how auto/biographical research can be used to 'give a voice' to people with learning disabilities. Auto/biographical research, in my terms, includes work with individuals on their biographies, or life stories, and oral history projects with groups of people to develop individual and collective accounts of past lives and events. In later chapters, I draw on my own Past Times project to illustrate the possibilities – and the pitfalls – of auto/biographical research.

The aim of this book is to look critically at the uses and limitations of auto/biographical research: in particular, to look at how it can be used to enable people with learning disabilities to speak for themselves about their own lives and experiences (and thereby help to set the record straight) and how it can also be used to encourage a greater historical awareness and understanding of past events. If the approach works, then there is at least the possibility that some of those 'lost' or 'silenced' voices of people with learning disabilities will be heard at last.

2 Research issues

Auto/biographical research can 'give a voice' to people with learning disabilities. In so doing it can enable people who are otherwise invisible and silent to speak about themselves and their lives. But how does this happen? How do people get a voice? And, when all is said and done, whose voice is it?

Three recent developments, in particular, have been important in enabling people with learning disabilities to speak and be heard: refinements in qualitative research; the growth of self-advocacy; and the burgeoning interest in oral history. The means by which people get a voice helps determine how that voice is presented, and who hears it. Sometimes other voices – not least those of researchers and writers – are heard instead. Nevertheless, changes have occurred and here I want to look at how it has become possible in recent years for people with learning disabilities, after years of silence, to begin to speak for themselves at last. Later in the chapter I will consider *whose voice* is heard, and why.

Getting a voice

Research is always about a process just as much as it is about a product or outcomes. In learning disability research the process is a complicated one because it involves people with little or no recourse to the written word and, for some, with few spoken words at their disposal either. It was widely assumed, as we saw in Chapter 1, that people with learning disabilities had little or nothing of interest or value to say about themselves or their lives. The means by which they come to speak, and the circumstances in which they are heard, are thus important factors in research.

The developments in qualitative research, self-advocacy and oral history have each been important in enabling people with learning disabilities to speak for themselves about their own lives and experiences. I propose to look at these developments in turn.

1 Research interviews

Qualitative research methods were popular in the USA in the early years of this century, in the era of the 'Chicago School', 1910-40. They declined in the 1940s and 50s in favour of the 'grand theories' of sociology, and the use of quantitative methods in the social sciences, until their gradual re-emergence from the 1960s onwards. This re-emergence did not, on the whole, touch the closed world of learning disability. After all, research interviews required the active involvement and participation of their interviewees and, for many years, it was widely assumed that people with learning disabilities could not be those active research subjects.

That assumption was widespread but not universal, and two studies stand out as exceptions to the rule of non-involvement of people with learning disabilities. The work of Robert Edgerton (1967, 1976), and the work of Robert Bogdan and Steven Taylor (1976, 1982), were exceptional for their time. These researchers actually interviewed people with learning disabilities, and sought their views about their lives. This approach was otherwise unheard of. Other research studies on learning disabilities did not look for or feature the views of the people most centrally concerned. Far from it. As Bogdan and Taylor (1982) pointed out, people with learning disability were rarely, if ever, approached for their insights into their own situations. Instead they were studied as 'a separate category of human beings' (1982, p. 7).

These pioneering studies made their mark. Clearly people with learning disabilities could be involved in research which was about them and their lives. Research interviews could be used to elicit their views. In the 1980s, a handful of researchers published papers on various aspects of face-to-face interviews with people with learning disabilities. (See, for example, Sigelman *et al.*, 1981; Wyngaarden, 1981; Flynn, 1986; Atkinson, 1988.) This 'modest flowering of papers' (Walmsley, 1994) reflected the fact that, increasingly, researchers were using interviews, and other qualitative methods, with people with learning disabilities.

Some researchers were successfully adapting research interviews into informal and largely conversational formats so that people with learning disabilities could feel relatively relaxed and unthreatened (Flynn, 1986; Atkinson, 1988). Other researchers went further in making the contact between researcher and interviewee as relaxed and informal as possible. For example, Jahoda *et al.* (1988) spent time getting to know people outside and away from the research project, and Edgerton (1984) used a 'naturalistic' approach with his respondents, spending time relaxing with them on social visits and trips out. Getting to know people by 'being there' with them, during ordinary and often boring days, was used by Julie Wilkinson (1990) as a means of capturing the experiences of people with learning disabilities at first hand. The in-depth interviewing approach used by Tim and Wendy Booth in their study of parents with learning disabilities (1994) involved them in spending a lot of time with their respondents, getting to know them and listening at length to their account of their lives. These refinements in qualitative research methods over the years have paid off. The sensitive use of interviews with people with learning disabilities, and the efforts made by researchers to spend time relaxing with their interviewees outside the research, have succeeded in giving people a voice. This is no mean feat – from having no voice for most of this century people with learning disabilities now have a voice, and an audience, through other people's research projects.

2 Self-advocacy

If some of the recent qualitative research studies are about giving a voice or granting an audience to people with learning disabilities, then self-advocacy is about people finding/getting a voice for themselves. It is an important recent phenomenon. Mostly, people with learning disabilities have begun to find a voice through self-advocacy groups (Crawley, 1988). The number currently involved in self-advocacy is an impressive, estimated 5000 (Mitchell, 1997). The growth of self-advocacy has paralleled the development of research studies which aim to include the views of people with learning disabilities. Jan Walmsley (1995) suggests this parallel development is not coincidental.

The original People First group was established in London in 1984, and the first newsletter was produced in 1985. The early days of self-advocacy were occurring at the same time as the growing interest in research studies which included the views of people with learning disabilities. Participative research and self-advocacy were parallel developments and were, presumably, linked. This was a two-way link. On the one hand, it could be said that self-advocacy influenced researchers, who now knew that people with learning disabilities could express their views, and wanted their voices to be heard. On the other hand, it seemed that self-advocacy was influencing people themselves, some of whom came to realise the value of research, and became more confident about taking part.

One cannot prove a causal connection between self-advocacy and research. One can, however, point to current research by people with learning disabilities as evidence of a connection. (See, for example, Whittaker *et al.*, 1990 and Minkes *et al.*, 1995.) In the wider disability field the connection is

15

that much stronger, and there are examples of research by disabled people which is associated with user movements (Oliver, 1990; Morris, 1989, 1991). In the absence of similar work by people with learning disabilities, they remain, on the whole, still subject to being represented by others, including researchers: *given* a voice, *granted* an audience.

Self-advocacy has, however, led to some important publications not least by People First: *Oi, it's my assessment* and *Everything you ever wanted to know about safer sex* (People First, 1993). These publications were created by and directed at people with learning disabilities. Also, there have been a number of chapters in books co-written by people with learning disabilities; for example, Etherington *et al.*, 1988; Amans and Darbyshire, 1989; Davis *et al.*, 1995; Downer and Walmsley, 1996. As conferences which address issues of interest and concern to people with learning disabilities now include people themselves as speakers or delegates, so conference reports are increasingly including the voices of people with learning disabilities: for example, *Speak Out with Other People*, 1992, Islington Disablement Association and *Women First*, 1993, Nottingham Advocacy in Action (Walmsley, 1993).

Whatever its links with research, self-advocacy has meant that many people with learning disabilities have begun to speak up for themselves, Again it is hard to prove a causal connection, but alongside the growth of the self-advocacy movement has been a steady stream of *autobiographies* by people with learning disabilities. They represent the clearest and most direct means by which people can account for their own lives. It could be said that the autobiography is the ultimate means of self-representation.

3   Oral history

The relatively recent, but quite rapid, development of oral history as a means of researching and documenting the ordinary lives of ordinary people has been an important step forward. As Joanna Bornat (1989) points out, the recollections of the 'famous, rich and influential' have always been considered worth hearing. Not so ordinary people – and even less so marginalized people or minority groups. Bornat calls the growth and development of oral history a 'social movement'. It allowed the voices of working class people, women, and people with learning disabilities, for example, to be heard and documented often for the first time.

In this social movement, historians became interviewers, and ordinary people became the source of often undocumented history about family life, working life, neighbourhoods and communities. Oral history was given further impetus by the growth of community publishing from the early 1970s, which meant there was an outlet – and an audience – for local historical and biographical accounts (Bornat, 1989).

On the face of it, oral history as an approach, and as a means of presentation, has much to offer people with learning disabilities. It has the potential to provide the forum in which people can speak about their individual and shared histories. It is a method, *par excellence*, of documenting the remembered and lived accounts of people with little access to the written word. It is a means by which they can reclaim their history. Other groups (women, lesbians, Jewish women, for example) have similarly reclaimed their own histories, and this has proved to be of 'symbolic and practical significance to oppressed and marginalized groups' (Bornat and Walmsley, 1994).

On the whole, people with learning disabilities have no access to or understanding of their own history. And yet there is a great value to people when they do have that understanding. It helps make sense of individual lives and experiences, especially lives lived as labelled and stigmatized, often segregated, people. Without access to history, people with learning disabilities are denied access to 'a sense of what has contributed to stigma, exclusion and marginalization' (Bornat and Walmsley, 1994). One way of gaining access to history is through sharing memories and, in so doing, beginning to understand more broadly how the past has shaped the present. This can also have the effect, according to Bornat and Walmsley, of affirming the validity of the communities to which people with learning disabilities belong.

The social movement which Bornat identified has largely passed people with learning disabilities by. Although there are many examples of locally published oral history accounts of local lives and communities, these do not – as Bornat (1992) found in her survey of 50 publications – include the voices of people with learning disabilities. They are 'invisible' people within local communities because they are not recognized as members of those communities and because they have been, and are, systematically excluded from ordinary life.

Oral history certainly has the potential to enable people with learning disabilities to have a voice, and begin to reclaim, and understand, their history. But it has not happened, and probably will not happen, through local community-based projects. Instead, oral history needs to be harnessed in separate settings where people have more of an opportunity to represent themselves. This approach has also worked with minority ethnic groups (who also are often not represented in accounts of community life) where a 'separate reconstruction' of past events becomes possible (Bornat, 1992). A similar separate reconstruction has been used as a means by which people with learning disabilities can tell their stories of exclusion and reveal details of their personal histories. According to Bornat (1992), 'invisible people' re-emerge in the telling of their own stories.

17

There is a danger in the 'separate reconstruction' that only differences emerge. This would recreate the situation that Bogdan and Taylor (1982) and Joanna Ryan (1980) have highlighted so well, where we tend to look only at how people with learning disabilities differ from us and not what they share with us. Researchers and interviewers need to be aware of their own personal and historical interests, lest they focus too one-sidedly on people's distinctive experiences as labelled people (Bornat and Walmsley, 1994). Oral history has proved effective and useful in reconstructing the history of a long-stay institution from the recollections of 17 of its residents (Potts and Fido, 1991). In the Past Times project, which is featured in detail later in this book, I made a conscious attempt to focus on ordinary and everyday experiences rather than only on those experiences which had marked people out as different.

Oral history has, in the past, had other limitations. One of these was the one-off nature of accounts, which had meant there was no opportunity for re-thinking or revising (Bornat, 1992). One-off accounts tend to be based on 'public accounts' (Cornwell, 1984); the more rehearsed and typical stories. Only later, when it is possible to tell stories at greater length, do fuller and more frank accounts emerge, those much more 'private accounts' of people's lives. The opportunity for a group of people to work together on a separate reconstruction over time means that public accounts can become private accounts. The Past Times project used time in this way. Over a period of two years people were able to revisit their accounts and revise them. They could, and did, add more private accounts. The project showed that history – personal or shared – does not just emerge ready made, it needs to be worked at and worked on over time.

Whose voice?

The question of 'Whose voice?' is relevant in learning disability research, perhaps more so than in any other area. This is because, as we have seen, people with learning disabilities are particularly prone to the (mis)representation of others. The developments of the last 15-20 years have given some recognition and value to their self-representation. Even so, it is still necessary to look at these developments, and the accounts which emerge from them, and to ask 'Whose voice?' is speaking.

Interviews have been adapted and refined in work with people with learning disabilities so that they now provide a very useful research tool. Biographical details of events and experiences, and views about aspects of their lives, can be sought with reasonable confidence from people with learning disabilities. This is what I refer to here as biographical research. It involves the researcher in the collection, compilation and analysis of personal testimonies. These may start off as autobiographical accounts by people with learning disabilities, but in an edited and collected form, or as illustrative quotations to shed light on the researcher's main themes, they become more biographical than autobiographical. In fragmented form, these accounts cannot hope to capture a full picture of the people concerned. Nor is it intended that they should. They are more likely to convey what is *different* about the lives and experiences of people with learning disabilities in some wider account or argument about the devaluation and marginalization of an oppressed group.

Whilst it is true that such arguments need to be made, the focus on differences does mean that commonalities between people are likely to be lost or diminished. Even more likely to be omitted are the ordinary and everyday events and experiences of life, the personal but mundane details of a life lived, which are at the heart of the autobiographies generated by people with learning disabilities themselves.

The voices of people with learning disabilities are certainly heard in biographical research but they are heard in an edited form, and are placed alongside other voices. The researcher's voice necessarily has prominence in the overall account; this is, after all, their work and these are their findings. And it is important to know about *oppression* and how people cope with, or have coped with, institutional life, poverty, deprivation, abuse and discrimination. (See, for example, Flynn, 1989; Booth and Booth, 1994.) Told in the words of people at the receiving end, these biographical accounts have the capacity to bring home the stark reality of people's lives. On this basis, people with learning disabilities may well be portrayed as vulnerable people, as victims of uncaring or exploitative systems. And it is true, they are. But they are more than that, and in their own accounts people with learning disabilities see themselves as more than victims. Do they know that they may be seen by others primarily as victims? Is this what they would want? Whose voice counts?

It is the autobiography which holds the greatest potential for self-representation, and for the authentic voice of the subject to be heard. And yet, even here, it has to be said that relatively few people, with or without learning disabilities, can write their own autobiography unaided. This applies to people in all walks of life, including people in the public eye, but it applies especially to people with learning disabilities. They have little access to the written word and, sometimes, they may struggle with spoken words too. A potential autobiographer, whoever they are, may well need a 'ghost writer' to work with or for them, but an autobiographer with learning disabilities may need 'a facilitator, an interpreter *and* a scribe' (Atkinson and Walmsley, 1997). So even in the realm of the autobiography we need to ask *whose voice is it?*

This question applies in relation to people with learning disabilities but does not usually arise in relation to the autobiographies of famous people, even when they have been written by ghost writers. This is because the writer has been commissioned to do the work, but the ownership remains with the autobiographer. In this way, we can distinguish between the autobiographies of people with learning disabilities which have been initiated, commissioned/written and owned by them, and the biographical accounts, which we looked at above, that form part of someone else's research story.

The voice differs depending on whether it is an autobiography, or a biographical account, but so too does the narrative style and content. Elsewhere I have suggested that 'true' autobiographies (written or initiated by people with learning disabilities) 'dwell on the *ordinariness* of people's lives, however extraordinary the settings or circumstances might be', whereas edited biographical accounts written for or about them dwell on those features which mark them out as *different* (Atkinson and Walmsley, 1997).

There are relatively few autobiographies written or commissioned by people with learning disabilities. Probably the best known is Joey Deacon's story, *Tongue Tied* (1974), which was also made into a television play. This is a particularly good example of someone who decided to write his own life story. As he was unable to write, and had difficulty in speaking, Deacon could only produce his book with the help of three friends who were also long-stay residents in St Lawrence's Hospital. They formed a writing team and the autobiography was written in a slow, laborious and painstaking way. In spite of Deacon's personal and social circumstances at the time, his account is primarily about the nice and ordinary things in his life – family, friends, holidays, birthdays and so on – and not about the segregated world of the long-stay hospital.

There are other examples of autobiographies by people with learning disabilities: *The World of Nigel Hunt* (1967); *My Life Story* (1991) by Malcolm Burnside; and *Mabel Cooper's Life Story* (1997). An important recent example of a collection of life stories or autobiographies is the anthology *'Know Me As I Am'* (Atkinson and Williams, 1990). This is important in that it includes the work of around 200 contributors and it is through their own words, or images, that people with learning disabilities portray themselves as fully rounded and complex human beings.

They emerge as more than the victims of oppressive and segregated systems. They are people with distinct personal histories and a wealth of experiences to draw and reflect on. Together the anthology contributors bring out the differences *and* the commonalities between their lives and ours, and they include the ordinary, the everyday and the mundane, as well as the stories of loss, separation and segregation.

The autobiographical voice

Autobiographies are important. They do more than give a voice to people with learning disabilities; they give that voice social, political and historical credence. This is because autobiographies have the potential to provide an *insider view* of people's real lives; to give us an *holistic view* of people; to provide a *counterbalance* to other views; and to form the basis of a *political document* for understanding and change. I will look at each of these aspects of autobiographies in turn.

The autobiography, according to Bogdan and Taylor (1982), allows us an insider's view of people's lives, a way in to an understanding of the groups or subcultures of which the autobiographer is a member. This point is echoed by Paul Thompson (1988). We cannot get an insider view by any other means than by developing a relationship with the person which is close enough to allow us to empathize and understand, and to see the world – and its institutions and agencies – from that person's point of view.

We also get a more 'holistic view' of people through an autobiographical account (Bogdan and Taylor, 1982). It allows us to see where we have things in common as well as where our experiences differ. We can get a fuller account of people's lives, and the complexity of their lives, and have access to their feelings and thoughts. An autobiography allows people to put their past into perspective, to make sense of their experiences.

Autobiographies act as 'a counterbalance' to other accounts (Williams, 1993). Often these other accounts have focused on pathological differences or deficits/defects or, through case records, have given a very limited view of people's lives. The autobiography allows for a richer and more rounded account. Fiona Williams (1993) also suggests that autobiographies act as a counterbalance in other directions too – tempering the professional orientation of normalization, for example, and 'the 'victim' approach of many of the well-intentioned revelations of the worst aspects of institutional life' (1993, p. 57). It is my contention that autobiographies are also a counterbalance to a whole set of victim accounts, many of which are now based outside institutions.

An autobiography, according to Bogdan and Taylor (1982), becomes a 'political document' when it is written. This operates in two ways. The autobiography as a document has an impact on its reader. It allows us 'to distance ourselves from our own prejudices' so that we can empathize with the person and see the world from his or her point of view (1982, p. 17). This distance allows us to stand back and reflect on our own preconceived ideas and assumptions. The second way in which the autobiography is a political document is that it has the capacity to relate to the experiences of other

21

people – and can influence them. This includes the academic community of researchers and teachers, but also includes people with learning disabilities. Atkinson and Williams (1990) make this point:

> Autobiographies and life histories create the opportunity for experiences to be shared, for common interests to be fostered, for common understandings to be forged and for consciousness to be raised. In this way they help to shift the burden of problems away from the individual who suffers them and on to the society that imposes them (p.8).

Auto/biographical voices

In a sense, the autobiographical voice is the voice of the self-advocacy movement. The person who 'speaks up' may also become the person who 'writes up'. The single autobiography has the capacity to influence its readers, and collected life stories have the potential to become not only political documents but also an important source of history 'from below'.

Autobiographies, however, tell the story of individuals, They do not tell the stories of groups of people or communities, or collect together the shared memories of times gone by. The approaches developed in oral history are relevant here, for they allow us to hear the individual speak but to do so within a social and historical context – and alongside the voices of others. This is where my own research comes in. The Past Times project includes the voices of individuals, but they speak as members of an oral history group. And there is my voice too, for in working with people, transcribing their words and assembling a collective account, this is also my story.

This approach is *auto/biographical*. It has things in common with biographical research (it aims for a collection of lives, and reflects multiple voices, including the researcher's), and with the writing of autobiographies (everyone gets to tell *their* story). But it is also different – it tells the stories of individuals, but does so against the social and historical backcloth of their time. The Past Times project is auto/biographical, and so too is the work of Potts and Fido (1991) who worked with 17 residents from a long-stay hospital to chart their lives as individuals but, at the same time, to tell the story of the institution itself.

Auto/biographical research has the capacity to combine the political document with the historical – to reflect the lives which have been lived, but to see beyond the individuals to a wider view of learning disability. Auto/biography contains many voices and tells stories at different levels.

3 The research

I want to turn now to auto/biographical research in practice, and to use my own research project to illustrate some of the possibilities of this approach and – inevitably – many of its pitfalls. I have referred to this project already as the Past Times project. It was not called this at the time. Then it was simply referred to as the 'history group'. Its revised title reflects the title of the book which came out of the project, and it now provides me with a quick and convenient shorthand way of referring to my own research.

At the end of Chapter 2 I suggested that auto/biographical research, such as the Past Times project, is able to combine individual life stories, or autobiographies, with multiple voices in order to create a collective account. It uses oral history techniques, such as reminiscence and recall, but also draws on the universal topics of life history work to enable individuals to tell their own life stories. If it works well, auto/biographical research has the potential to enable people with learning disabilities to tell their stories against the backdrop of history.

The origins of an idea

My starting point with the Past Times project was primarily to explore the use of oral history techniques with people with learning disabilities. I wanted to see if these techniques, and this approach, would work with older people with learning disabilities. The use of recall and reminiscence with older people generally has been well documented over the years (recent examples include Coleman, 1986: Bornat, 1989; Gibson, 1989; and Fielden, 1990). However, documented accounts of the use of similar approaches with older people with learning disabilities are still very rare (one such example is Potts and Fido, 1991).

My interest in exploring oral history techniques had its origins in two earlier projects. One project was a follow-up study of people with learning disabilities who had moved out of long-stay hospitals in Somerset to live in the community. This research involved me in interviewing 50 people in their own homes (Atkinson, 1988). I was pushed for time and had to rely on one-off interviews with everyone. This was far from perfect but it allowed me a glimpse of what might be possible. I was convinced by this experience that people with learning disabilities do have stories to tell. More work was clearly needed to enable them to do so but at least they were emerging as legitimate interviewees.

The other project which had influenced me was the collection and compilation of the anthology of poetry, prose and painting by people with learning disabilities *'Know Me As I Am'* (Atkinson and Williams, 1990). The work involved in co-editing the anthology had demonstrated that life story, and oral history, work with people with learning disabilities was not only possible, it was able – perhaps uniquely able – to tap a rich seam of memory and experience. It looked as if this sort of in-depth work with smaller numbers of people might generate as much, if not more, material than my single interviews with 50 people in my earlier project. The anthology had involved me in collating, selecting, editing and commentating but not in the actual work of interviewing people or working alongside them in life story or oral history work. This was my starting point. I wanted to have a go, to be that person who enables others to speak out about their lives.

I was also responding to the last sentence of the anthology, intended as our clarion call to others to go and do likewise: 'There are more stories to be told and voices yet to be heard' (Atkinson and Williams, 1990, p. 244). This turned out to be my inspiration. I wanted to listen to those voices and, in working with people to compile their stories, to enable them to be heard beyond the world of learning disability.

The written word is important in this society. It is, it seems, of particular importance to people who have little or no access to it themselves. One of the simplest yet most striking accounts in the anthology is by Doreen Cocklin who marvels at the sight of her own words: 'This is the first time anything I have said has been written down' (Atkinson and Williams. 1990, p. 168). The anthology itself, as a collection of (often oral) accounts of the lives of people with learning disabilities, has proved to be the source of pride and celebration for its many contributors.

My oral history project was set up with this in mind – it was to be oral in the sense that people would be encouraged to talk, but it would also lead to their stories being written down. This is where it became more truly auto/biographical. The anthology contributors had each received personal copies of the book in recognition of their work. Similarly my Somerset respondents had each received an illustrated booklet of the research findings as a personal keepsake of their involvement. I planned from the beginning, therefore, that the people involved in the Past Times project would likewise receive a written product at the end. I was not sure what form this would take but I envisaged that any emerging stories would be compiled into some sort of small booklet. This was not the main aim of the project itself – as I saw it then – but more a secondary aim, a by-product of our joint exploration of oral history techniques. This was not what actually happened in practice. In time the book itself became the primary aim and driving force for the people concerned. But that's another story, and one which I will come to later.

Aims of the research

Although my initial aim in this research was to explore a method, to see if and how oral history approaches could be used with people with learning disabilities, I also wanted to hear the stories which would no doubt unfold. More than that, as I explained above, I anticipated those oral stories would become documented stories.

But this was also a history project. I wanted to know about individual lives, but to know them in a social and historical context. This was my other primary aim: to collect narrative accounts of people's lives against the background of key legislative and policy changes in the learning disability field. I would be working with people with learning disabilities – as I saw it – to construct a history 'from below' (Humphries, 1984). This could include, for example, the effects of the eugenics movement, and the incarceration of people in institutions. It could include exclusion from the educational system, and its consequences for individuals, and it could include the more recent move to community care, and the impact this might have had on people's lives.

This aim was tempered by my wish to represent people as social and historical beings in the widest possible sense. This was to be a history project, but a history of sameness and commonalities as well as a history of differences. Thus I invited people to remember the ordinary and everyday experiences of their lives, to recall happy memories as well as sad ones, and to see their lives as part of the unfolding and wider history of this century.

These were complicated and, to some extent, conflicting aims, and they led to a complex project. The trouble was that not only did my aims conflict with each other, they also at times conflicted with the shifting aims and wishes of the group members. Some of these conflicts have only come to light with the benefit of hindsight and through a process of critical self-reflection. It was difficult, if not impossible, to pinpoint them during the course of the project.

There were all sorts of reasons for this difficulty, and some of them will become apparent in the course of this chapter and the two which follow.

The project was already complex in what it set out to do. It became ever more complicated because I chose to work with a group of people rather than using individual interviews. The choice of a group format was made with the best of intentions, and it reflected my aim that people should have the opportunity to share their memories and work towards a collective account as well as develop their individual life stories. Again I had been influenced by my work on the anthology *'Know Me As I Am'* in making this choice. This was because the anthology had demonstrated in various ways the 'richness, depth and diversity of people's memories', and had gone on to suggest that 'much social history, particularly of long-stay hospitals, still remains to be told from "below" and "within"' (Atkinson and Williams, 1990, p. 243).

Although most contributions to the anthology had come from individuals, a noticeable number had come from groups, such as the 'Women's Group' and the 'Experiences of Handicap' group. What was particularly striking was that whilst many individual accounts were told in rich detail and depth, the group accounts actually went a step further. They were able to incorporate commonalities as well as differences; to develop shared insights and a measure of understanding; and to allow readers a glimpse of a hidden world.

The potential of groups to use shared memories as a basis of insight and understanding is echoed by Paul Thompson (1988) in his discussion of the use of groups more generally in life history work. There is very little written, however, on research work which involves groups of people with learning disabilities. An earlier project of mine had included research interviews with people living together in group homes, but these were with mini-groups of householders (Atkinson, 1988, 1989). A more effective, but still quite limited, use of group interviews, in combination with individual interviews, was reported by Jan Walmsley (1990) in her account of her work with members of a self-advocacy group. At the time of planning the Past Times project, therefore, there was little practical guidance to draw on. I set out with high hopes but no map of where I might be heading. My idea was to provide a supportive group setting where individual life stories could be recounted. This was meant to combine two approaches in one: to aim for the richness of individual accounts, but to do so within the more insightful and reflective mode of a group setting. This was no easy task. Our journey to an unknown and uncharted destination proved to be a hazardous one at times.

Meeting the group

I wanted to work with a group of people with learning disabilities, not an existing group, but one brought or coming together especially for this project. My first task was to find and recruit some group members. Although my initial idea was to try and recruit older people with learning disabilities living in the community, and not necessarily in touch with learning disability services, it was quickly discounted as impractical. How could an outsider, such as myself, hope to make contact with people not using services?

My next and more realistic idea was to make contact with potential group members via local learning disability services. The local social services department gave me the go-ahead to get in touch with two likely sources of interested people. One was a residential home for older people in Dunstable where some ex-residents had been re-settled from a local hospital, and the other was an adult training centre in the same town where a pre-retirement class was being run with some of the older clients. I visited both places and made contact with potential members via two key intermediaries (staff members at the two settings) who later joined the group themselves. They introduced me to people who they thought might be interested in the project. The rest was up to me – and to them.

I met people informally and casually to talk about what I had in mind. I met everyone individually, rather than together, and said I was hoping to form a history group. I introduced myself as someone from the Open University who was interested in history, and who was thinking about writing a book on historical events. Their memories of times gone by would be an important source of information for this book. I invited people personally to join a series of group discussions based on their memories of past events and experiences. Seven people decided to join on the basis of this introduction and explanation. Two more people applied to join within the first month, having heard about the history group (as it was by then known) and deciding for themselves that they would like to be members. Their request to join seemed at the time an important validation of the group, and its focus. They remained members throughout the whole two-year life of the group.

The group thus consisted of nine people, seven men and two women. The age range was 57-77 years, with most people in their late 60s or early 70s. Group members had at least two things in common. Firstly, each person was currently linked with special day and/or residential services so that everybody already knew, or knew of, at least one or two other members of the group. Secondly, group members were all living in Bedfordshire and seven (of nine) had always done so. The same seven people had lived for much of their lives in long-stay hospitals. The county address proved to be a bit of a tenuous link as, in their younger days, people had lived in different towns and villages in Bedfordshire. The hospital link did prove important, though, as it led to the sharing of many memories of institutional life.

The project spanned two years, although it was never intended (by me) to last so long. Indeed I had assumed it would last about six weeks. The group's life was extended because it quickly became apparent that it provided a forum where experiences could be remembered, re-lived and shared. The weekly, and later fortnightly, group meeting quickly became a popular event in people's lives. It gave them an opportunity – which they grasped – of recalling, and reflecting on, important aspects of their personal pasts, and of making sense of those experiences. The group format made possible the sparking-off of individual and shared memories between people.

The group met on 30 occasions and all the hour-long meetings were, with permission, tape recorded and transcribed. In working on this project together, the nine people concerned have defied the labels which over the years have sought to define who they are and how they should live, labels such as 'mental defective', 'subnormal' and 'mentally handicapped'. In this project they became oral historians.

In the book of the project, *Past Times*, group members are listed as contributors. Perhaps one of the best ways of 'meeting' them is through the potted-biographies which each person – this time on an individual basis – prepared with me for the book. These brief entries (see below) are written in the present tense. They capture group members as they were in 1993, when *Past Times* was privately published (Atkinson, 1993a). They are snapshots in time. The rest of *Past Times* is about who group members were – and how they were seen – over all the rest of the years of their lives from childhood to adulthood.

Bert Angell lives in a residential home for older people in Dunstable. He likes to get out and about, and enjoys visiting the local pub, lunch club, library and cricket ground. He is a member of the RSPB, and a playing member of a local bowling team. He is studying cookery at a college in Luton, and is already an expert pastry cook. He is keen on sport, especially cricket and football, but also enjoys having a small bet on the dogs and horses. His other interests include gardening and steam trains.

Bill Baker lives in a residential home for older people in Dunstable. His main interest is in gardens, especially flowers. He used to be a keen gardener, but nowadays has to pursue his interest through looking at gardens, visiting the garden centre and looking at gardening books from the library. He loves flowers, and enjoys sitting in the gardens of his home.

George Coley lives in a residential home for older people in Dunstable. He enjoys playing cards, dominoes and snooker, and watching football, rugby and horse racing on television. He also enjoys a drink at his local pub.

Edna Day lives in a hostel for people with learning disabilities in Dunstable. She regularly attends a local social centre for retired people where she enjoys dancing, bingo and basket work.

Margaret Day lives in a hostel for people with learning disabilities in Dunstable. She is keen on knitting, sewing and embroidery and enjoys watching television, especially comedy programmes. She likes to go out for a walk, and enjoys an occasional drink at the local pub.

Albert Gaylor lives in a residential home for older people. He likes to get out and about, and enjoys visiting his relatives for lunch, playing cards at his lunch club and having a drink at the local pub. He is studying an Art and Design course at a college in Luton.

John Rivers lives in a group home in Luton. He regularly attends a social centre for retired people where he enjoys doing basket work and indoor gardening. He also likes to go for walks in the nearby park to look at the flowers, and to take trips into the town on the bus to look at the shops. He is a regular Church-goer and a keen spectator at the home matches of Luton Town football club.

Denzil Smith lives in a hostel for people with learning disabilities in Dunstable. He enjoys walking, and often walks into the town centre to look at the shops. He also likes trips to the library, garden centre and pub. His favourite holiday is staying with his brother in Ireland.

Brian Sutcliffe lives in a group home in Leighton Buzzard. He is a keen gardener, and is currently on a two-year work placement as a gardener. He also enjoys planting flowers in the beds and containers at his home. He likes going to the pictures, playing bowls and collecting model vintage cars and buses. He loves trips on steam trains, and he collects posters and books about them. He also likes watching television.

(*Past Times*, pp. 86-87)

The researcher's role

I set out, as I saw it, to test a method, to record people's stories and to begin to co-construct history from below. I quickly found, however, that there was more to telling, and hearing, the stories of people's lives and experiences than simply providing the time and space. The researcher's role was central. It seemed to have a bearing not only on how stories unfolded, but even helped determine what they were about.

In retrospect this does not seem surprising. If a research interview is a social situation, influenced by the perceptions of its participants, then a group is an even more complicated social situation. As well as the interpersonal dynamics which operate in one-to-one encounters, there are the baffling undercurrents of the group dynamics to contend with and counter. I met these unspoken forces and, through a process of reflection, I later came to understand them. But I did not recognize them at the time. After all, I had invited people to talk to me about their memories. There I was with my tape recorder, and my questions, all I had to do was switch on and record history.

Well, it was not like that at all. The research project was auto/biographical: it contained several voices, including mine. This book reflects those different voices. Although in a sense it is 'my story', I also include other people's stories so that they can represent themselves and, to some extent, stand outside and be separate from my account. Much of my story is about the research *process*, and how the group members came to tell their stories. But it is also an account of my own involvement in the process and how – usually unknowingly – I helped influence its direction. How I presented myself, and how people saw me, appear in retrospect to have been important factors in determining how we got on together, and in shaping what happened. The trouble was, I did not know this at the time. After all, I had a research project to run.

1 Evidence from elsewhere

There is, of course, considerable interest in the qualitative research literature about the interpersonal dynamics of research interviews and other encounters. Although I was quite familiar with this literature beforehand, I found that it was one thing to read about the need for self and other awareness in the quiet safety of a library and another thing to apply these ideas on the spot to a large and lively group – and at the same time to reflect on my own part in the process. The ideas themselves are sound. The question is, how does one apply them except in retrospect?

The Past Times project drew on many of the ideas around in 1990, particularly in relation to participative and feminist research. Much of the concern expressed in the literature was on how to avoid using or exploiting already vulnerable people in the interests of so-called research. This had led in some quarters to a conscious move away from the hierarchical relationships which were said to characterize more traditional research methods (Oakley, 1981). Instead, some researchers were calling for the ever greater involvement of research participants in studies which were about, or impinged on, their lives (Holman, 1987; Graham, 1984). Much work had been done on using research interviews as opportunities for people to talk about themselves in an atmosphere which was friendly and enabling. It seemed that most people, given such an opportunity, actually welcomed the chance to talk to an attentive and interested listener about their lives and experiences. Sometimes, though by no means always, this was found to be an uplifting experience which gave people a sense of self worth (Coleman, 1986).

One way to avoid exploitation was, it seemed, to involve people actively in the research process in just the way I had envisaged for the Past Times project. There was more to it than that though, because ever closer involvement and contact between the researcher and 'the researched' carried with it the possibility of a different sort of exploitation. Thus even the consciously non-exploitative approach, which aimed to build trust between the researcher and the participants, was itself suspect. This was because the creation of an atmosphere of trust, the development of a relationship between 'equals' and the blurring of distinctions between the people concerned, could lead participants to expect a continuing friendship and a continuing place in the research project. And these were false expectations. They could lead in the end to a sense of loss or betrayal when the research relationship was terminated, and the researcher moved on (Finch, 1984; Patai; 1991), often with the research (Stacey, 1991).

What to do? In order to enable people to relax and talk freely about themselves, there is a need for closeness. In order to avoid one sort of exploitation in research, there is a need for the active involvement of participants. But closeness and involvement set up expectations which may yet turn out to be exploitative. I aimed in my research for closeness, trust and involvement. I also raised expectations about continuity and friendship. The group lasted two years partly because, having made it a success, I did not have the heart to stop it. And its members wanted it to continue, perhaps forever.

Unless all research is to stop forthwith, there has to be a way through these contradictions. One way is to remember that the research experience can be, and often is, a positive experience for its participants. Balanced against that knowledge is the fact that there may well be those pitfalls outlined above to contend with, and safeguards may be needed in order to avoid the worst of them. Self awareness, and an awareness of the interpersonal dynamics of the interview situation, may help, including the recognition that this may well prove to be an 'emotionally charged' situation for a participant receiving undivided attention (Patai, 1991). Such awareness is not always possible at the time, as I have discovered, so my emphasis has tended to be on making sure that, overall, the research experience is seen as enjoyable, and that it carries with it a sense of achievement rather than loss.

Qualitative research, especially where relationships are nurtured and prolonged, can take on aspects of the psychoanalytic or psychotherapeutic process. This means that strong feelings may be unleashed and these may need careful and sensitive handling in order to ensure a positive outcome. Life history and oral history work, in particular, can incorporate the therapeutic effects of remembering, and opportunities to reflect on a personal past can lead to a stronger sense of self in the present (Thompson, 1988). The feeling of being affirmed and validated in the research process can be further developed through the 'product' of the research, especially if the product is a publication which gives people a voice. This is what I tried to achieve with the production and private publication of *Past Times*.

2 My agenda

As I suggested earlier, one of my primary aims in the Past Times project was to explore with the group history from below. This is why I dubbed it the history group and invited older people with learning disabilities to join it. The one thing they all had in common was that they had each been identified at some point in their lives as a 'person with a learning disability', or a predecessor label. The other thing that most of the group members had in common was that they had lived for much of their lives in long-stay hospitals. I knew this in advance of the project but I felt that it would be inappropriate to use that prior knowledge to invite people to talk at the outset about their experiences of labelling, segregation and hospitalization. We would get there but we would get there by a roundabout route. The direct approach to history was out on two grounds.

I ruled out the direct approach primarily because, at the time, it seemed to be a high risk strategy. There was an obvious risk to the people concerned. Supposing they readily joined in with the recounting of their experiences as labelled people and, in the course of it, got in touch with long-hidden feelings of frustration and anger. What then? Another risk, as I saw it then, was to the project. I did not want to burn my bridges at the outset by upsetting people unnecessarily. Supposing group members were horrified at the prospect of revealing painful memories to a stranger and to each other, and as a result refused to do so. Perhaps they would never come back. The whole project could fold.

The other reason for ruling out the direct approach to recounting the history of learning disability was that it focused too much on *difference*. I was looking for a fuller picture of people's lives than a series of accounts dwelling on how different their lives had been from everybody else's. There were, and are, plenty of research projects which do that; this one, I hoped, would instead balance oppression with the ordinariness of everyday life. I wanted to know about differences, but I also wanted to know about commonalities. And I decided to start with commonalities – differentness could come later.

Thus I chose what seemed at the time the safest, and most principled, course of action. I intended to avoid early and direct questioning about group members' specific experiences as people who had been labelled and, as a result, had been segregated in special settings for people with learning disabilities (or 'mental defectives' in the old terminology). These experiences had included, for almost everyone, quite extended periods of incarceration in long-stay hospitals. Instead of focusing on the experiences which they shared, and had in common with each other, and which were quite different from my own, I decided for all the reasons outlined above to focus on ordinary memories. I chose to focus on the normal life course, using universal themes, such as childhood, home life, schooldays, families and neighbourhoods. My starting point was with 'normal' life and 'typical' experiences. My plan was to concentrate in the early days of the group on drawing out those memories which they had in common with other people rather than dwelling on their differences. We would approach those differences only when we were ready for them.

That was the plan, and I was happy with it. It reflected my interest in, as well as my commitment to, the whole person rather than the victim. It would, I felt sure, enable people to relate to, and engage with, memories of a universal kind, and there was no doubt in my mind that a richer and more rounded history – and histories – would emerge as a result. At the same time I was being protective of everyone, including myself – protecting us from the risk of too-early disclosures, and sparing us from endless depressing accounts of life in institutions. These would emerge, I hoped, in the fullness of time.

This was my agenda. In the end it worked, but not in the way I had imagined when I planned the project. Whilst Brian was only too happy to describe his back-to-back house in Yorkshire, and the cobbled streets of his home town, other people's memories of their families, and their childhood homes, were inextricably linked with memories of earlier loss, separation and rejection. My focus on childhood, and other early memories, inevitably led to the disclosure of painful memories. It had to. Ironically, by way of contrast, people's later memories of their adult life in an institution, because they were shared, were often told with humour and in a spirit of defiance. What I had overlooked in my careful planning was that personal memories of an unhappy childhood can actually be more painful than shared memories of adult life in a long-stay hospital. In reality I could not protect people from their own pasts. Nor should I have tried.

3 Starting out

Prior to our first meeting, I drew up a list of themes to explore within the group. The list was compiled with the help of two colleagues and with reference to various sets of guidelines on the best ways of doing reminiscence work. (There are various such publications available now. See, for example, Humphries, 1984; Thompson, 1988; Gibson, 1989; Humphries and Gordon, 1992). Oral and life history work, as well as actual reminiscence groups, aim to involve people in recalling their early memories of childhood, family life, schooldays and so on. My list of topics was similarly intended to transport people back to when and where they were born, and to the circumstances of their infancy, childhood, adolescence and adulthood (see Figure 3.1). The group did not see this list; these headings were a reminder to me of the universal themes I wanted us to focus on in the early weeks of the group.

Basically my idea was to draw people out on the sort of houses they had lived in as children, and where they were situated; what their neighbours and neighbourhoods had been like then; and how they had cooked, taken a bath, washed and kept warm. I also hoped to find out about families; family size and composition; family relationships; and the everyday details of mealtimes, chores and discipline in the family home. I aimed to uncover personal memories but also period details of the time: descriptions of the clothes people wore, for example, and what happened at home on wash-days.

At each group meeting I was accompanied by one or two staff members from the residential or day settings who knew at least some of the participants well. They took their cue from me, pursuing and reinforcing the topics chosen from my list. They joined in with their own reminiscences, which was particularly helpful as that meant, to some extent, they acted as role models for everyone else. Their willingness to join in, and review their own lives, almost certainly encouraged other people to do likewise. They were helpful to me in other ways too, particularly in drawing people out and helping to translate and interpret their responses.

My own task, as I saw it then, was to provide a safe and friendly environment in which people would feel free to talk about their earlier life

34

experiences. My role was that of a friendly, if slightly distant, group facilitator. I was there to ask questions and to reflect on what was said, but not on the whole to join in with the reminiscences. The idea was to spend time in the early group meetings on what I had identified as 'safe' topics. Spending time in this way would not only enable people to gain confidence in themselves, but would also encourage them to trust me and each other sufficiently to allow them to confide more personal memories later.

Childhood memories of:

* **Family**
  Who lived at home?
  Work or unemployment
  Family mealtimes
  Jobs and chores
  Outings
  Rows, arguments
  Pets
  Childhood illness or accidents
* **School**
  Primary school
  Secondary school
  No school
  Special school
  Boarding school
  Playtime
  Homework
  Friends
  Bullying, teasing
  Punishments
* **Religion**
  Church, chapel
  Salvation Army
  Sunday school

* **Food**
  Mealtimes at home
  School dinners
  Eating out
* **Shops**
  Corner shop
  Butcher's shop
  Pawnshop
  Department stores, clothes
    shops
  Markets

* **Home**
  What sort of house?
  Where?
  Rooms? own room? bathroom?
  Keeping warm
  Washing and ironing
  Bath tubs and wash basins
  Lights, lamps and candles

* **Fun and Games**
  Toys
  Games
  Sport
  Circus, fairground
  Birthdays and Christmas
  Conkers
  Bonfire night
  Sweets, comics, pocket money Picnics
  Park

* **Transport**
  Walking, cycling
  Scooters and motor bikes
  Pony and trap
  Motor car
* **Clothes**
  Casual clothes
  School uniforms
  Caps and hair cuts
* **Major events and headlines**
  General strike
  Depression
  Second World War
  Coronation
  World Cup

Adolescent memories of:

* Leaving school
* Girlfriends/boyfriends
* Employment
* Leaving home
* Having fun
* Family and friends

Adult memories of:

* Girlfriends/boyfriends
* Employment
* Leaving home
* Having fun
* Family and friends

Figure 3.1   List of themes

I saw myself as 'responsible' for this group in every way imaginable. It had, after all, been set up at my instigation, and it reflected my aims, agenda and assumptions. To cope with this sense of responsibility I tried to exercise some sort of control over the group, and its workings. I had chosen the 'safe' topics to explore; next I attempted to influence the group's agenda. I tried to, but failed. I reckoned without the commitment and sense of ownership of everyone else in the group. It wasn't mine to control. It was theirs.

4   The group's agenda

My control was always tenuous. I would bring up topics and persist with them, sometimes against all the odds. At times this was fine, and they would strike an answering chord in somebody. But often they did not. Instead group sessions often left me feeling out of control and powerless to influence their direction, as group members effectively sabotaged my chosen themes. They did this in all sorts of ways: cross cutting conversations, critical side commentaries, stage whispers, loud yawns, interjections from the floor and the accomplished telling of extended anecdotes (on rival topics).

In spite of the mounting evidence to the contrary, I continued to see myself as potentially powerful in that setting. I knew that many of the group members – if not all – had encountered powerful women in their lives before, and I assumed, therefore, that I would be seen by them as one more in a long line of potential and actual oppressors. I had done all I could to counteract this image. I had set up a 'safe' group, and had chosen 'safe' topics. I was informal and friendly. Ironically, I think I succeeded, except in my own eyes. Group members, I think now, actually saw me as I intended them to, as a friendly and interested person. Unfortunately I didn't believe this myself. I feared that, through a process of transference, they would continue to see me as a powerful person. With the benefit of hindsight, I can now see that group members actually believed what they saw, and related to me at times as their confidante, a kind of 'benefactor' in Edgerton's terms (Edgerton, 1967). But my powerful woman image stayed with me for a long time and helped determine the fact that the group and I proceeded along different, though linked, pathways. We met up later, but it took a long time.

In retrospect, it seems obvious that group members had role models other than the powerful woman image. She was my problem not theirs. Instead they related to me as their 'benefactor' in a variety of ways. Sometimes I was a friend, sometimes a co-conspirator, and sometimes just a 'young woman' who was interested in their stories. In the event I was more likely to be teased than deferred to, patronized rather than looked up to and even flirted with rather than feared. Nods, winks and smiles turned out to be more the order of the day than anxious looks.

Group members' individual perceptions of me as basically a friendly person led, to my surprise, to early and even cheerful disclosures about their lives. In the first three meetings, for example, even though I was persisting with my 'safe' topics, group members themselves tried to introduce a range of 'unsafe' areas. These included being 'put away' as children; abuse; separation and loss; deaths; and admission to hostels and hospitals. Whatever happened to picnics and playtime? Group members were, it seemed, far more interested in revealing their personal pasts than in building a joint history of earlier times. The latter was my agenda.

People in the group were, from the outset, open about themselves and only too willing to share painful memories. Their agenda, it seemed, was to talk about, and make sense of, their personal pasts and histories. In the next chapter I will look at some of the things involved in this process of life review.

4 The process of life review

The Past Times project was not set up to enable people to engage in a process of life review. Rather, it was set up by me to test a method, to provide an opportunity for stories to be told and to co-construct an historical account of learning disability in the twentieth century. Some of the confusion which ensued in the group's early life can probably – in retrospect – be attributed to the co-existence of, and the conflict between, two agendas. My agenda was to pursue my research aims. The agenda of the group members was to look back, and reflect, on their past lives – to undertake a life review. This was not articulated by them, nor was it understood by me until long after the project was over. And yet the evidence is there, on the audio recordings and in the transcriptions; group members consistently tried, often against the odds, to recount and reflect on their own personal stories. They wanted not just to tell their stories, to order, but to review their lives.

The opportunity to review one's life is important. Ruth Finnegan (1992), for example, suggests that the telling of 'personal narratives' can actually help people 'validate' their lives and make sense of their various life experiences. Similarly Birren and Deutchman (1991) report how the telling of their life story helps older people develop greater understanding and self worth, through enabling them to gain a sense of perspective on their life. They make the point that in the later years of one's life, in particular, it is important to feel that one's life has mattered, that it has had a purpose or made an impact on the world.

Other writers and researchers have made similar points. Paul Thompson (1988), suggests that the act of remembering one's own life is crucial to a sense of self, and Peter Coleman looks to the life review as a means of maintaining one's identity. In Coleman's view, the life review allows someone to understand the negative experiences on their lives better; to draw lessons from them, and thus to feel more whole and integrated (Coleman,

1986). The sense of personal identity comes with the overview of one's past life and achievements, and the recognition of the value of the life lived.

These claims look very convincing: life review is seen as a means of self-validation, and a way of developing self worth, a sense of self and personal identity. People positively welcome – if not actively seek out – opportunities to make sense of their lives. That much is obvious. What was not obvious to me at the time was that a group of people, brought together for a set of research aims – which included telling their stories – would want to focus right from the word go on that one aspect of the group's intended work. There was no problem in exploring a method; this group of older people with learning disabilities were more than willing to speak out about their lives. That was exactly what they wanted to do. My attempt to focus on universal themes and commonalities between people, and my wish to develop a collective account, were, in the early months of the group, bound to founder. I did not know that at the time. What seemed like resistance to, or sabotage of, my agenda was actually a counter-drive towards a process of life review.

This chapter looks at that process of life review. It did happen. I could not stop it. It is a tribute to group members that they persisted with what was important to them.

Revealing personal pasts

In all, the group met on 30 occasions and all the hour-long meetings were tape recorded and transcribed. As well as an opening session, where group members met one another and began the process of recall, and a closing session where goodbyes were said, there were two main phases in the group's life. The first phase (15 sessions) was predominantly the life review phase. The second phase was predominantly the collective oral history phase (the subject of Chapter 5).

Of course, it was not as neat as this in reality. Lives were reviewed throughout, although there was a clear difference in how this was done. The first phase saw very personal accounts emerging; the second phase saw them being revisited and reconsidered within a more sweeping overall story. The first phase also saw some shared memories of the social and historical period emerging, but these had their basis in personal memories of home and childhood. With these caveats, it is possible to locate the process of life review as characterizing the first phase of the group. It was at that point, at the end of what turned out to be the first phase, that I produced the first slim draft of *Past Times* and, albeit unwittingly, transformed the group's dynamics into more of a shared endeavour than purely a set of individual accounts. But more of that anon.

As I explained in detail in Chapter 3, my intention in the early days of the group was to introduce shared themes of a universal kind for people to relate and respond to. My initial list of themes included memories of childhood and adolescence in terms of *who* group members lived with (family life and relationships); *where* they lived (type of house and neighbourhood); and *what* life was like (home, school and community life). Discussion of hospital life, in particular, I proposed to leave until later in the group's evolutionary cycle.

In this phase I saw myself primarily as a researcher, relating to individuals but within a group setting. What this meant in practice was that I addressed group members rather than the group as a whole, asking questions, seeking clarification and reflecting back people's answers. Not surprisingly, this phase of the group's life was characterized by group members, on the whole, speaking directly to me rather than to each other. They might also address the one or two staff members who regularly attended the group, especially if I was having difficulty in understanding what they were saying.

The following exchange is taken from the transcript of the second meeting of the group. It amounts to a question-and-answer session between myself and several members of the group. From time to time, staff members try to help out when understanding breaks down. My question was 'Can you remember which year you were born?'

Extract 1

Bill:	1920, I was.
Dorothy:	1920?
Bill:	Yeah.
Dorothy:	Right....[Writes] Brian, what were you saying? February? You got as far as February. Do you know which year?
Brian:	Erm...
Anne (Staff):	Let me just think, I'll try and work it out.
Dorothy:	Right. Anybody else know what year they were born? George?
George:	May 15th, 1913.
Dorothy:	You're 1913. Anybody else? Can you remember which year you were born? Bert? Albert? Do you know how old you are? Then we can work it out ....
Albert:	Mm.
Bert:	No.

Dorothy:	Does anybody else know? George, do you know which year Albert was born?
Denzil:	I was born on a farm.

(Tape transcript, meeting 2)

This was an awkward, fact-based question-and-answer session. They were not all like this! In fact, the main characteristic of this phase of the group was the willingness, readiness even, of group members to talk about their individual and personal pasts. The types of memories varied, and included some period details of the time. I will come back to these memories again later. Suffice it to say here that although people were drawing on their personal memories of their own childhoods, the net effect is a collection of wide-ranging memories of coal fires and candlelight, childhood games of marbles and hopscotch, descriptions of wash-tubs and mangles, and many other features of everyday life in the early and middle years of this century.

The surprise came for me in the other sorts of memories which were revealed in this first phase of the group's life. This happened from the very first meeting, and it continued whenever the opportunity arose – usually in the spaces between my universal themes and safe topics. These other memories included the disclosure of painful or traumatic events in people's lives. The following extract is also taken from the transcript of the second meeting. It illustrates the readiness with which group members revealed their personal pasts. In this example, George and Brian reveal their earliest memories of death. These confidences are directed at me, not at the rest of the group.

Extract 2

George:	[Interrupts].... I had one little brother, but he died.
Dorothy:	You had a young brother did you, George?
George:	Yeah, he died.
Dorothy:	How old was he then? He died as a child?
George:	Well, he died in his mother's ....you know ....
Dorothy:	As a baby?
George:	Yeah.
Dorothy:	Oh, that was sad. Any other brothers and sisters?
George:	No.
Dorothy:	Just the one?
George:	Only one, yeah.

Brian:	.... one brother and three sisters. I used to have a younger brother, but he died, in the water. He got drownded, he did.
Dorothy:	He got drowned?
Brian:	Yes.

(Tape transcript, meeting 2)

This exchange was actually unprompted by me. It happened at the instigation of first George, and later Brian, and came out of a discussion about family size and composition. The exchange was highly relevant but unexpected. I thought we were on a safe topic, simply counting up the numbers of brothers and sisters. This was a case of two agendas conflicting again.

Conflicting agendas

The first phase of the group was characterized by this conflict of the two agendas – mine, to pursue a normalization line, tracing ordinary lives and everyday experiences; and group members' own individual agendas to talk about, and make sense of, their personal pasts and histories. I was the researcher; the instigator of the group and initiator of the project. I was responsible, as I saw it, for the group and its members. This sense of responsibility prompted many of my actions and reactions during the early months of the project.

I felt responsible, inappropriately as it turned out, for protecting people from their own pasts and their personal feelings. This was expressed through my safe topics policy. I also felt responsible for the atmosphere in group meetings, and I tried to set an informal tone, a light touch, so that people would feel comfortable, relaxed and valued. I felt responsible for the continuity of discussions and saw it as my job to keep conversations going. So it was that, in the early days at least, I introduced the themes on my list and, as these ran out, I acquired various reminiscence aids such as audio tapes, slides, photographs and other memorabilia – such as cigarette cards – to use as memory triggers. And that was not all. I also felt responsible for holding the group together, keeping it a pleasant place to be and finding ways of keeping everybody's interest alive. And later on, as we got deeper into people's autobiographical accounts, I duly felt responsible for the therapeutic – or otherwise – effects of such revelations. I tried to make sure that group members were not overwhelmed by sadness or regret.

This was a lot of responsibility, and it weighed heavily on my shoulders. It also impeded my capacity to be open to what was really happening around me, to such an extent that I misunderstood what people said, missed cues to continue or to stop, overlooked clues to the meaning and significance of stories, and misinterpreted what I thought I had heard. My perception of my role, and the tasks I had set myself, often conflicted with what other people perceived as my role and tasks. These perceptions helped determine how we related to one another.

Of course, my role was a contradictory one – to facilitate the telling of stories but, at the same time, to keep to firm boundaries around the content and direction of those stories in order to 'protect' people. I tried to be both the group's facilitator *and* its protector (a point I have made elsewhere: Atkinson, 1993b). This meant that my role switched between opening up and exploring some topics and, at the same time, ignoring and closing down others.

This is illustrated in the next extract (Extract 3), again taken from the transcript of our second meeting. My theme was 'What sort of house?' and I pursued it regardless of Edna's mention, first, of her mother's death and, second, of going to live in a hostel.

Extract 3

Dorothy: Right, so if you can all think back to when you were children; can you remember what sort of house you used to live in?

Edna: I used to live up Farley Hill with my mum before she died.

Dorothy: And what sort of house was that?

Edna: Well, a big one.

Dorothy: A big one?

Edna: Yes. A big one, up Farley Hill, yes.

Dorothy: Up Farley Hill.

Edna: Yes.

Dorothy: Was that in . . . .?

Edna: In Luton, yes. Then I had to come to the hostel.

Dorothy: Right. And can you tell me about the house? What was it like?

                        (Tape transcript, meeting 2)

Looking back to that exchange between us, I can now see that Edna's agenda was to review the events in her life. She was ready to talk and more than prepared to reveal personal details of her past life – the trouble was, I was far from ready to listen. The need to make sense of the past is clearly a strong motivating force. Not only Edna, but other people too in the early days of the group, struggled to have the personal details of their lives heard and acknowledged.

And yet, at the same time, I was trying to facilitate the telling of stories. I was using my checklist of themes to draw people out, so that their stories unfolded in a particular way. This was meant to be facilitative – and, of course, protective. As no one else had access to my checklist, the only way I could pursue its themes was by asking lots of questions. As a result I often felt like 'an interrogator' (Atkinson, 1993b). Although I wished the exchanges could be more like conversations, I was driven into the questioning mode by my feelings of responsibility for the group, and its members. It was not necessarily the most facilitative approach, however, a point I have reflected on elsewhere: 'Yet on those few occasions when I said something simple and personal ("I was never very good at skipping") it became more like a conversation ("Poor Dorothy!" "Oh, what a shame"), and moved the group on'(1993b, p. 65).

My other task, as a researcher, was actually to hear what was said. This should not be underestimated. A combination of dental neglect, especially the lack of dentures, strong regional accents and unclear speech meant that I was often unable to understand what people were saying at the time. Sometimes their meaning only became clear afterwards with the constant playing and re-playing of the tape. Sometimes it never became clear. I attempted to deal with this, as far as I could, by reflecting back to people what I thought they were saying. This was intended to clarify meanings there and then, but, failing that, I would have a second chance later when I transcribed the tape. In reflecting back I was talking to the speaker at the time, and other group members who were listening, but I was also talking to myself on tape.

Reflecting-back is a technique borrowed from counselling. It is meant to be a means of enabling people to gain awareness and insight into their situation and circumstances. Used by me as a way of talking to myself outside the group, however, had the unintended consequence of closing some of our conversations down. Such exchanges could lead nowhere, as the following extract illustrates.

Extract 4

Dorothy: What sort of gardening did you do, John?

John: I used to work on the proper garden.

Dorothy: The proper garden?

John: In the greenhouse and that.

Dorothy: So you worked in the greenhouse . . . .

John:	I did a lot more than that.
Dorothy:	More than that?
John:	Yes.

(Tape transcript, meeting 19)

So I had my agenda, usually reinforced by whichever staff members were present, but group members had their own agenda – to undertake a life review. This was never articulated directly but took shape in various ways. Edna, for example, pursued her own personal agenda as determinedly as I pursued mine. In Extract 3, above, she tried to talk about her mother's death and how she had to move into a hostel. That was in the group's second meeting. In our third meeting, Edna tried again as the following extract (Extract 5) illustrates.

Extract 5

Edna:	I used to live with my mum and then she went out one night, and she got knocked down by a car, so she had to go to hospital to have cataracts on her eyes and then she died.
Dorothy:	Oh dear.
Edna:	But I used to do all the housework and everything, do her shopping for her, go out with her every Saturday night.
Dorothy:	What sort of age were you then?
Edna:	I was only younger.
Dorothy:	You were younger than you are now?
Edna:	Yes.
Dorothy:	Were you a very young child? At that stage. Or was that later?
Edna:	No, that was when I was fourteen.
Dorothy:	Right. So when you were very young, did you have your own room? Because you were a very large family, from what you were saying last week . . . .
Edna:	Yeah, I can't remember, 'cos I was put away, see.
Dorothy:	Yes, I remember that . . . . Can anyone else remember? Did you have your own room?

(Tape transcript, meeting 3)

Unfortunately for Edna, her agenda conflicted with mine. My theme was 'Did you have your own room?' and this was pursued in spite of Edna's revelations of her mother's accident, operation and death, and how she herself had been 'put away' as a child. Edna tried to continue her own theme in spite of my questioning on a different tack. That was one way to resist. There were two others; one was a retreat into silence and the other was to hold the floor long enough to bring out and explore a rival theme.

Although Bill revealed a lot about his home and family in later meetings, he was reluctant in the early days to respond to close questioning on the subject. This was an evident source of pain for him, as it later became apparent. In the extract below (Extract 6) he retreats almost into silence. He is too polite not to answer at all, so instead he stalls. He blocks our well-meaning attempts to draw him out.

Extract 6

Janet (Staff):	Did you have any brothers and sisters, Bill?
Bill:	I don't worry about them.
Janet:	Did you though?
Dorothy:	[....] Can you remember your neighbours, Bill?
Bill:	What?
Dorothy:	Who used to live next door?
Bill:	No, no.
Mo (Staff):	[....] You were telling me this morning how old your mother was when she died . . . .
Dorothy:	How old was she?
Bill:	I can't tell you.

(Tape transcript, meeting 2)

So much for safe topics! The least safe topic for Bill was the subject of his childhood, and especially the loss of his family. He actually returned to it two sessions later, when he felt the time was right. This was unprompted. In fact, the rest of the group were talking about scrumping apples.

Extract 7

Bill:	[Interrupts] My mother died when I was 10, it was a shame. It was her chest. I had a big family, but I don't worry about them. I forget how many. I lived at school, at Kingsmead School, I got visited once a month. Dad was in the army, then

46

he was a car park attendant. He used to come to see me once a month.

(Tape transcript, meeting 4)

The other way to resist my agenda was to hold the floor with an extended anecdote. I described this elsewhere as 'a fine narrative tradition' (Atkinson 1993b, p. 66). Whoever regaled the group in this way held the floor, and became the temporary leader – determining which themes were to be talked about and deciding the direction of the group's discussion. Two people, in particular, vied with each other, and with me, to determine the group's agenda. They told long stories; I asked questions.

The stories were well told, and held their audience as the speaker intended. The well-told anecdote became a tradition in the group. George and Brian, and sometimes Margaret, were its main exponents. The following tale from George about his schooldays is a typical example of the genre in its early days of use in the group.

Extract 8

George: We had slates and chalk at school. When you got older you had pencils and a pen. I don't know if John's ever done this, but we used to get some ink on some paper and flick it at the teacher. 'Course he'd be writing on the board. 'Who did that?' he'd say. 'Course, nobody spoke! We'd all sit there, writing. He'd say, 'I'll find out who's doing it!' One of the boys went and told him, 'So and so's done it.' Then he'd clip you one behind your earhole.

(Tape transcript, meeting 5)

Public and private accounts

One of the distinctions which emerged over time, and which could be seen in retrospect, was between the public and private accounts as told by group members (Atkinson 1994). The process of life review in the group meant that some autobiographical details could be talked about early on because these were already public accounts. Only later could hitherto hidden layers of more private accounts be revealed. (The distinction between 'public' and 'private' accounts was made by Cornwell, 1984.)

Group members were motivated to tell their stories. This operated from the outset. I have already indicated how readily people talked about seemingly

47

once traumatic events in their lives. What only became apparent later in the group was that there were other, more private, stories behind these relatively public statements. The distinction that applies here is, I think, between a more rehearsed account, by which I mean one that has already been told and re-told over time, and can be readily shared, and the even more personally revealing, and unrehearsed, accounts of the past, the truly private accounts. These are not readily shared. They emerge later.

This is not to minimize the personal meaning, and power to move, of the public accounts, nor to underestimate the impact of remembered events. Even these public accounts were, as we have seen, based on memories of what must have been, at the time, painful or tragic happenings in people's lives. The process of telling and re-telling over time, the opportunity to reflect and re-consider past events, seemed to have taken away the immediacy of the pain, and allowed some sort of protective distance to form. The later unrehearsed accounts, the private accounts, 'still had the capacity to conjure up, and convey to others, the remembered pain' (Atkinson, 1994, p. 99).

The process of life review started with these public accounts. They were an important staging post in the process. They provided accounts which could be built on later. Edna's life review began with revelations about her mother's death, and how she herself was 'put away' in a hostel. The next extract (Extract 9) is where she returns to the theme of loss and separation. This is also taken from the transcript of the second meeting.

Extract 9

Edna: And then, of course, I was put away because of my father, because he was no good. I got put in a children's home.

Dorothy: Your father was no good?

Edna: Yes. When I was a little baby, I got put away.

Dorothy: [Quietly] Oh, I see.

Edna: He was no good.

Dorothy: That's sad. What was wrong with your dad?

Edna: Well, he used to go out drinking every night and, erm, he used to hit my mother.

(Tape transcript, meeting 2)

It is difficult to see this as a public account because it is so painfully revealing. And yet, it seems to have that status. The private account lies in the detail behind the headline events. They come later.

Not everyone was so revealing in their accounts. The group contained members who were very reticent about their lives. At a later stage in the cycle of group meetings, therefore, I suggested that we do some small-group work. I thought this would give the quieter members more of an opportunity to have their say. And so it did. But it did something else as well: it allowed everyone – including those who had spoken up from the outset – to move from public to private accounts. The real revelations came out in these small, more private sessions. This was life review in action.

The switch in approach thus had unanticipated, but beneficial, consequences. The procedure for two or three meetings was that we would gather as the whole group first, to say 'hello' and make contact again. We would then spend the better part of the session working in pairs or small groups of twos and threes, with each pair, or mini-group, being accompanied by myself or a staff member. At the end of the hour we would meet up again altogether for a cup of tea and a chat.

The more personalized contact which the pair/mini-group format allowed led to the revealing of more layers of memories, including those of a deeper and more intensely private kind. These hitherto unrevealed, and unrehearsed, private accounts still had the capacity to recreate some of the pain that had been felt at the time. In a very real sense, the pairs and mini-groups enabled group members to recall, re-live and reflect on key events in their past lives. This was truly an opportunity to look back at, and make sense of, some of the lived experiences behind the headline events of the more public accounts. The process of life review, in this group at least, seemed to need both sorts of accounts.

Although an accomplished narrator of the extended anecdote in the overall group, George used these quieter moments to talk about the things that really mattered to him and which still hurt. It was only in the mini-group that he revealed the hidden story of his early family life, as the following extract (Extract 10) illustrates.

Extract 10

Dorothy: So your mother used to do the shopping?

George: Yeah, yeah.

Dorothy: In the village?

George: I think I was better off without her. She didn't like me, I don't know why. Me dad and me were just the opposite, I got on well with him.

Dorothy: And with your mother?

George: She used to hit me, knock me around. I used to come home
               from school, and if anyone had come with me, a little boy or a
               little girl, and we'd had a bit of fun, she'd say: "I'll deal with
               you!"

                                                   (Tape transcript, meeting 13)

Commonalities and differences

Of course, my emphasis in the earlier phases of the group's life was on the
'normal' life course. My checklist took us through themes of a universal kind
such as childhood, home life, families and schooldays. My starting point was
with normal life, ordinary living and typical experiences – with a view to
drawing out those memories which group members had in common with
other people, rather than forever dwelling on their differences.

This approach worked well in that many individual and shared memories
emerged of rural and urban working class life in the early and middle years of
this century. There was a lot of enjoyment, not least for myself and staff, in
being able to recall, and share with everyone else, the rich details of the bath
times and bedtimes of childhood. Commonalities did emerge. People's
memories converged. In the following extract (Extract 11) Brian recalls with
relish the family washday in his Yorkshire home.

Extract 11

Brian: We did our washing down the cellar. We used to have a stone
               sink down there. We used to have an old mangle machine, and
               a tub for your clothes. We used to poss' em in, peg 'em up.
               We used to put a line across the street and hang our clothes
               out.

                                                   (Tape transcript, meeting 15)

I return to the theme of commonalities, and shared memories, in the next
chapter. Here I want to turn to differences because members of the group had,
on the whole, led far from normal lives and consequently had enjoyed few of
life's typical experiences. They were single and childless. With one
exception, they had lived in institutions for long periods of their lives. They
had mostly been excluded from paid employment. The memories of group
members were, thus, quite different from the experiences of most people of
their age and class.

50

The sense of difference was apparent to all of us. Group members articulated it; they had, after all, experienced and felt it. They were all too well aware of the points at which their lives diverged, and were different, from other people's. Thus even a celebratory account of a remembered achievement, such as getting a job, was likely to contain a discordant note in how it had ended with the sack.

Everyone, at some point in the project, revealed painful memories from childhood. This was in spite of my safe topics/universal themes philosophy – childhood was, of course, the source of much pain. The painful memories were around the themes of loss, separation or rejection. Edna's early autobiographical revelations were based on such themes. In the following extract (Extract 12) John remembers the last time he saw his mother.

Extract 12

John: I never had a dad. I was at Girton in Cambridge, it was a home and school. I was eight. That was the last time I saw my mum. She used to write to me, the staff read them to me, the letters. My mum lived in Bedford by the river, in a home. I think she died in 1971. I didn't want to go to the funeral.

(Tape transcript, meeting 20)

Even Brian, who had lived with his parents well into his adult life, was aware of how his experiences were far from typical or ordinary. He had attended the local school as a child, but this had proved to be at some quite high cost to himself, as the following extract (Extract 13) illustrates.

Extract 13

Brian: I used to wear a dunce's hat. She used to put a big cap on my head and it said on the front 'Dunce'. 'Cos I couldn't write.

(Tape transcript, meeting 11)

Life review can be a painful process. It highlights differences between people just as much as it celebrates commonalities. And yet it is important. Group members took every opportunity, intended and unintended, to look back on their lives and remember past events. They were engaged in an essential task of later life – they were intent on making sense of their lives. And they did so in spite of my attempts to focus on similarities and shared experiences.

5 Compiling a collective account

One of my aims in the Past Times project was to work with people with learning disabilities to tell their stories, and to use these stories to co-construct a collective historical account. This was a dual aim. Although I hoped, ultimately, to look at where people's lives diverged from the typical life course and to explore those differences, my initial aim was to compile a collective account of ordinary lives based on shared memories of everyday life earlier in this century.

My checklist of themes was designed to tap into these everyday domestic and social memories. In spite of the conflicting agendas in the first phase between myself and the group – where I worked more towards a collective account and group members focused on the process of life review – the checklist worked to some extent and details of everyday life emerged. So although the first phase of the group was the life review phase, it did contain the beginnings of a collective account. It was only a beginning, however, as I had to struggle to keep to my agenda in the face of considerable resistance. Everything changed later in the group when the appearance of a first draft of *Past Times* signalled a shift in group dynamics, from individual stories to shared memories. I shall come to that story later in this chapter, but first I want to look at my earlier attempts to enforce a collective agenda on to people intent on looking back on their own lives.

Period details

One of my early themes was what sort of house, and home life, people remembered from their childhoods. A sub-theme was whether as children they would have had their own rooms or, as seemed more likely, they would have shared rooms – and perhaps beds – with brothers and sisters. This was a topic I pursued in the third meeting. In the extract below (Extract 14) some ordinary, everyday domestic details do emerge, but they cut across a much more serious memory from Margaret's childhood.

Extract 14

Dorothy: Can anyone else remember? Did you have your own room?

Brian: I did, yeah.

Edna: I shared with my sister, and then I used to go to bed with my mum.

Margaret: I don't remember anything!

Dorothy: Don't you?

Margaret: No.

Dorothy: You don't remember when you were a little girl?

Margaret: When I was a little girl I was put away.

Dorothy: Were you? Oh, I see. Ah. Erm. How old were you then?

Margaret: Fourteen and a half.

Dorothy: Before that, before you were fourteen and a half, were you living with you mum and dad then?

Margaret: Yeah.

Dorothy: And did you have your own room? Can you remember?

Margaret: Yeah, I had my own room.

Dorothy: Can anyone else remember? You were saying, Brian, that you had your own room when you were a boy.

Brian: Yeah. We lived in a back-to-back house, and the street was all cobble-stones. We used to put a washing line across the street, and hang washing in the middle of the road. We had a hook in the wall.

Edna: We used to have a copper bath for the washing. We used to do the washing in there.

George: It was hard work in them days.

(Tape transcript, meeting 3)

Luckily the drive to make sense of their own lives was sufficiently strong and enduring for group members not to be too easily diverted from their task. Looking back, it would have been all too easy for Margaret, and Edna before her, to give up on the idea of talking about, and reflecting on, their lives. It is

53

to their credit that they did not give up, but took what opportunities came their way to have another go. Margaret later returned to her childhood memories and told her story in full.

The tenacity on the part of the group members was, however, matched by my rather single-minded (as it now seems) determination to focus on similarities and shared memories. And so the striving towards a collective account continued even as I ran through, and then ran out of, the so-called safe topics on my original checklist. This was a matter of some concern, and I began to worry about how to keep the group going and how to maintain people's interest.

I tried a new tack. I looked for some external input which might stimulate discussion in the group – on shared memories, of course. This led to my recourse to reminiscence tapes, slides, photographs, cigarette cards and other period items. The reminiscence aids, as it turned out, (and much to my relief) were greatly enjoyed. They did, in fact, help bring out some of the commonalities between people's experiences. We could all, including myself and staff, join in the discussion with our own memories of mangles and marbles.

Something else happened, too, as a result of my recourse to reminiscence aids. In contrast with some of our earlier meetings, group members actually began to relate more directly to each other, as one person's memory almost inevitably sparked off somebody else's. Much to my delight, memories were shared, and some period details of the past were captured on tape. The following extract (Extract 15) is an exchange between George, Brian and Margaret which was triggered by a picture of an early model of a vacuum cleaner.

Extract 15

George: It's what you did the carpet with.

Brian: It's a vacuum cleaner, an old-fashioned one.

George: We didn't have one, we used a pan and brush. If we had to scrub the floor we used a bucket of water and a bit of soap. We used to scrub the floor on our hands and knees.

Brian: We had a bucket and mop.

Margaret: We used a brush and pan. We scrubbed the kitchen floor.

George: [Addressing staff] You younger generation, you don't do that today!

(Tape transcript, meeting 7)

In the first phase of the group's life, then, my emphasis was on the 'normal' life course. Reminiscence was directed, first, by my themes of childhood, home life, schooldays and so on, and then later, as I ran out of my own themes, by reminiscence aids which emphasized shared experiences and commonalities between people. The two approaches did lead to some sharing of period details. They did so sometimes, as I have demonstrated, at the expense of more personal memories. The collective approach sat very uneasily alongside the telling of people's own stories – in their own way and at their own pace.

Although this uneasy mix of agendas has become very apparent over time, especially when listening to the tapes of our discussions and – even more so – when studying the transcripts, nevertheless I did experience some disquiet at the time. I tried to pinpoint the source of the unease in the reflective diary which I kept throughout the life of the group. In an early diary entry (following our third meeting) I noted these following comments:

Extract 16

The method works. But how do I make sense of so many different contributions? No clear picture emerges. Am I spending too much time on specific, and focused, period details and not enough time on their own memories? I need to keep some sort of balance.

(Diary extract)

Such a balance proved elusive. The whole of the first phase of the group was characterized by the dual focus on individual and shared memories. Overall, I felt the balance swung more towards autobiographical accounts and became the life review phase. Although I kept my focus, and tried wherever possible to switch the discussion back to my safe topics and universal themes, nine determined autobiographers proved more than a match. But things did change. If phase one was predominantly about life review, phase two – which I inadvertently ushered in – was about compiling a collective account.

Changing the dynamics

The dynamics changed when I produced a first *written* compilation of people's stories. This marked the beginning of the second phase of the group's life, where 'the group became an entity, with a life and a momentum of its own' (Atkinson, 1993c, p. 205). This change began during the course of our first 15 meetings. As meeting followed meeting, and transcript followed transcript, it became apparent that in spite of everything, we had a product in the making. It was evident that stories had been told. Not only that, but they had been recorded on tape.

It was for this reason that we took a break from meetings during the summer of our first year. This gave me time to compile the fragments, vignettes and anecdotes into a collective and coherent whole. The account which emerged was a joint one, with individual and attributed contributions collected together under a series of themes such as 'Family memories', 'School life' and 'Home life'.

During this summer break I also toyed with the idea of transforming all the fragments into individual life stories. The result, however, seemed to distort the work of the group as a whole. Some individual stories were long and complex whilst others barely existed. This reflected the fact that three or four people talked a lot about themselves, and five people said relatively little. And yet these five people were clearly important as group members; they affirmed and validated other people's stories, they were an appreciative audience, and their own memories clearly resonated with those which were articulated by others in the group. Their individual life stories, as they had so far emerged in the group, could not convey any inkling of this level of involvement. As individuals they would vanish. As group members they had a vital part to play. For all of these reasons, I discounted the idea of 'reconstituting' individual life stories from childhood to old age. A joint account seemed far preferable. It would acknowledge everyone, however little they had said, and it would recognize all contributions as valuable and valid, however modest they might seem in isolation. The joint account also, of course, represented my agenda.

The compilation of stories resulted in a document which, to my surprise, was several thousand words long. This was clearly booklet size. The document was thus made into a large-print booklet. Its pages were stapled together and it was given a coloured cover. I gave it the working title of *Past Times*, and it was reprographed at the Open University for all group members, as well as a few extras for family, friends and staff. Thus it was that when we met again in the autumn of our first year, I was able to hand everyone a personal copy of the booklet. It became known simply as 'our book'.

The first draft (as it turned out to be) of 'our book' acted as a catalyst for a dramatic change in the group dynamics. At the very least, there was a change of ownership. My agenda was replaced by theirs – or so it seemed. This came as a great relief to me as it lessened, if not removed, my overriding sense of responsibility. This one act of reciprocity on my part changed completely the way in which we interacted within the group. The delight in the book as it was, and a shared desire to make it bigger and better, proved to be potent forces. What happened was that the book itself became a memory trigger, or prompt, to its various contributors, and I spent more and more of my time from that point on giving readings from its pages. As the readings continued over the months that followed, and the layers of memories steadily peeled away revealing private accounts as well as the more public ones, so 'our book' became 'our second book', and, finally, 'our third book'.

It was apparent, even at the time, that a major change had taken place in the group dynamics. The explanation, as usual, came somewhat later in the process. Looking back now, it seems that 'our book' was important in at least three ways. It was important as a *written* account of people's lives, a factor which I will explore in more detail in the next section of this chapter. But it was also important in changing perceptions within the group, and in changing the focus.

The impact of the first draft of *Past Times* was immense. It somehow made sense of the group and its work. For the first time we had something to show for all those meetings, all those words. Group members began to see me differently. I was seen as a useful person as well as a nice one. And this worked both ways. I now saw them as true oral historians, the 'custodians of valuable individual and social histories, but generous custodians who were willing to share their knowledge' (Atkinson, 1993b, p. 68). In retrospect, it seems that the work we did together subsequently on 'our book' was the coming together of our two agendas. We could now do both. We could pursue my agenda, to build a collective account and, at the same time, we could pursue theirs, which was to tell personal stories and reveal individual histories.

The first appearance of 'our book' was a turning point in the group's life. As I have suggested elsewhere (Atkinson, 1993c, p. 206), for 'our book' one could almost read 'our group', although no one actually articulated this thought. The coming together of fragmented pasts into a compilation of individual histories in 'our book' was highly symbolic. It suggested that the group itself had come together, and had become 'our group', with shared goals, a sense of identity and interaction between its members.

And so it was, then, that the second phase of the group's life was so strikingly different from the first. In the first phase, I was the instigator and the facilitator, and group members, on the whole, addressed me. In the second phase, the ownership of the project shifted, and I became its servant (Atkinson, 1993c, p. 206). Now group members spoke to each other as well as speaking to me, and collective memories began to emerge. Any support which was needed to cope with painful moments of recall was now as likely to come from peers as from myself or staff. The group, it seemed, had 'come of age', and was increasingly taking control of its destiny. And my role changed too. It had to. Now I had become, in effect, the group's scribe, and it was my job to listen, record, transcribe and write – and then to read out what we had written, thus starting the next cycle of readings-and-memories.

I will now illustrate some of the changes in the group dynamics which characterized this second phase of the group. The changed nature of group interaction, where members spoke to each other as well as to me, and where peer support was both offered and accepted, is illustrated below (Extract 17). This extract is taken from the tape transcription of the eighteenth meeting, where members of the group are recalling their war-time experiences. These were memories, for several people, of war time in Bromham Hospital.

Extract 17

George: They dropped a bomb, and it fell somewhere near Bromham.

Dorothy: Oh, I think I've got that story.

Margaret: Yeah, we see that, we see that bomb, it come over F1, and we was all in the cloakroom. We see this bomb go over the top.

Dorothy: Were you scared?

Margaret: No, I wasn't scared . . . .

Brian: Poor Margaret [He puts a hand on her arm].

Margaret: . . . . the board had come down from the window, so we put it back up.

Dorothy: Yeah, we've got a little bit about that in here as well, when the board came down.

George: I should think you remember it, don't you John? Do you remember that bomb that come down near Bromham when the war was on?

John: Yeah, in the cornfield.

(Tape transcript, meeting 18)

This extract also shows how interactions between people could easily lead to the sharing of memories. Although memories were deeply personal in the sense that it was individuals who remembered, and felt keenly, their own loss of home, family and friends, there was also a sense in which they were shared. At some level a personal loss was also a collective loss. This was because everybody knew, from experience, the causes of these individual losses. Long-term hospitalization brought in its wake separation from home

58

and loss of family, sometimes forever, and in their sharing of these memories, group members were beginning to reclaim a collective past.

In the extract below (Extract 18) Margaret talks about leaving home as a child. This story was clearly hers, but it resonated with the experiences of others in the group. Most people could identify with her story. Theirs might differ in its detail, but the sense of loss was shared.

Extract 18

Margaret: When I was a little girl I was put away. I was fourteen and a half. I went to Cell Barnes to live because they said I was backward. My dad refused to sign the papers for me to go, but the police came and said he would go to prison if he didn't. I cried when I had to go with the Welfare Officer.

(Tape transcript, meeting 16)

I will come back to the content of Margaret's story, and the stories of other members of the group, in later chapters. Here I want to keep the focus on the *process* of the work we did together in the group.

My task in this second phase was, in essence, to serve the group – to facilitate and record its discussions in order to enhance 'our book'. As group scribe I felt I had a socially sanctioned role. Better still was the fact that the group was now highly motivated to keep to its own task of revealing individual and shared memories. This meant that I could, at last, shed some of my earlier responsibilities. As memories grew deeper and became more painful, so it seemed that support and humour grew stronger within the group. I noted some of these changes in my research diary after the seventeenth meeting of the group. This was still quite early in the second phase of the group's life but already there was a sense of shared endeavour:

Extract 19

A good session. My tiredness evaporated as people came in smiling. No Bert, but Albert was there. Apparently he talks a lot *outside* the group nowadays. Bill returned! He looked fine considering what he's been through. He was in a wheelchair, but very active. He contributed a lot, especially about hospital days. [...] It was relaxed and fun. They were proud and pleased about how far they'd come, and how much they knew. It felt a good place to be! [...] They haven't made a formal decision, but maybe they don't need to. Maybe they're doing it by their commitment to the work in hand. Who's in charge? Not me, it seems!

(Diary extract)

59

The second phase of the project was characterized by a shared sense of group identity. This had found expression in the production of *Past Times* in its various drafts. This booklet had, at the same time, given symbolic recognition to the group. 'Our book' was a product of, and a spur for, 'our group'. As a group, people came to share common goals (to create 'a bigger and better book') and there was a shift to increasing interaction between members. My role was to write – and to read out – more than it was to lead and to facilitate. The telling of stories had passed into other hands.

Written lives

My original research aims had been met. The method had certainly proved viable with this group of nine people with learning disabilities. And, what was more, rich accounts of their lives had been told and recorded on tape. An additional and shared research aim had emerged in the second phase: that these accounts be transformed into a written oral historical account of group members' lives and experiences. This aim found expression in the book *Past Times* in its various manifestations. The written format proved to be of major significance to group members. Although most people were unable to read well or fluently (if at all), nevertheless they saw the written word as authoritative. It seemed that, somehow, their spoken memories were validated by being written down.

As people with learning disabilities, group members have always had restricted access to the written word. And yet there was no doubt that they recognized its value as a means of influencing opinions and shaping attitudes. The book *Past Times* was a motivating force. They wanted their work to be in print because they wanted other people to know about them and their lives.

The written word proved important in this context in three interconnecting ways: it was empowering, it was enduring and it brought understanding. The written word, of course, had started as the spoken word. But the words were spoken in a group, to an audience, and they were tape recorded. This gave group members the opportunity 'to participate' and 'to witness' (Diederich, 1994), to represent their lives in their own words. The spoken word became the written word, and this proved especially empowering. As Diederich has suggested, the written word helps to give meaning to the lives of people with learning disabilities, and enables them to be seen in a different way. There is a danger that 'without the written word their words are scattered, and heard as nonsense'. The group's own book, *Past Times*, gave something back to the people concerned; it allowed them an all-too-rare opportunity to feel a sense of ownership, a sense of achievement and a sense of belonging.

The spoken word has a transient quality and is 'unrepeatable' (Portelli, 1991, p. 279). Writing on this theme of transience Portelli suggests: 'The oral discourse "runs through our fingers", so to speak, and must be "solidified", "frozen" if we are to hold it, however precariously. Writing, on the other hand, literally fills our hands with solid, already-frozen words' (Portelli, 1991, p. 279). The written text has more status, in this society, than the spoken word and consequently was more highly valued in the eyes of group members. Part of its value is that it is enduring. Spoken words can float away. The written word endures indefinitely. Members of the group knew that, written down, their stories – indeed their lives – would also endure.

The written word can also lead to a greater understanding of one's own life – life review – within the context of other lives, and the social and historical context of the time. In the group, this process was facilitated by our readings. This was a way of revisiting lives, and reflecting on what had gone before. Stories could be confirmed, expanded and shared. New insights could emerge in the reading, re-hearing, and re-telling, of stories. This process of re-sharing and, sometimes, re-shaping of lives led to a greater understanding of personal *and* collective memories.

This growth in understanding through reflection, both individual and shared, is not unique to the Past Times group. Potts and Fido (1991), for example, also used readings as part of their oral history project. As they began to write the history of the long-stay hospital through the words of 17 of its older residents, they read out each chapter as it was drafted. Each reading stimulated more memories and more information. This led to an understanding of their own history, a kind of historical awareness. More than that was a wish for other people to know too: 'As people have talked, they have learned to value their own history and become increasingly confident and determined that the public should know what life has been like for them' (Potts and Fido, 1991, p. 12). In an educational programme with a group of Puerto Rican women, Rina Benmayor (1991) reported how the reading of autobiographical essays moved the discourse from an individual to a collective level. This occurred because the participants realised that their circumstances were not 'unique, accidental, or the product of their own errors or "shortcomings"' (1991, p. 162). They developed a social and historical awareness of their situations.

The written word helps enhance the understanding of those people who have been involved in its production. It can also enhance the understanding of others. Members of the Past Times group discovered this when they first showed our initial draft of the booklet to family, friends and staff. The next extract (Extract 20) is taken from the transcript of the seventeenth meeting. This followed the session when the personal copies of the first draft had been handed out, and they had been taken home for others to look at.

61

Extract 20

Margaret: They all looked in those books.

Dorothy: Oh, did they? Great.

Margaret: Yes.

Dorothy: What did they think of them?

Margaret: Jolly good.

Dorothy: That's good.

Janet (Staff): Yeah, I met one of the people that works at Margaret's place, in the supermarket, and we stopped and had a chat about it.

Ann (Staff): Yes, I think everyone is really interested.

Dorothy: So maybe we can think seriously about getting it published then, because this is just a temporary version . . . .

Brian: Yes, yes.

Dorothy: . . . . and we could do a nicer one. So that's a possibility.

Brian: We could make it bigger, and better.

(Tape transcript, meeting 17)

A collective account

'Our book' brought together our two agendas. It enabled group members to have their individual stories recognized in print, and those individual lives were seen within the context of other lives. The coming-together of individual accounts, in order to produce a collective account, happened in two ways. Firstly, the cyclical *process* of readings within the group served to confirm existing stories, and generate new ones. Secondly, the overall balance of accounts which make up *Past Times* means that the publication itself is the highly visible *product* of the group's work.

I had chosen a group format for my research, so that people could speak to, and listen to, others and so that memories could be shared. The group met together over a period of two years, so there was every opportunity for trust to develop between people. The regularity, and continuity, of the process of recall and reminiscence over time meant that stories could be told, reflected on and revisited. There was no danger, here, of the one-off interview effect in which stories are produced as 'snapshots' without the possibility of reconsideration and revision. Instead, group members could, if they wished, re-draft their stories in the light of further memories or thoughts, and re-tell them differently when the opportunity arose.

Such changes often came about through a process of reflection. This could happen even in an otherwise busy and lively meeting as some group members listened to others and, at the same time, reflected on their own lives and experiences. People could also, and often did, reflect on their stories outside the group, continuing to think about them between meetings. Lawrence and Mace (1992) make this point: 'The feelings which have re-surfaced in telling a story from years ago can be re-examined, while the teller listens to others talking, or goes home to think about it some more' (p.12). Group members, whether inside or outside the group, could thus mull over their story, or aspects of it, make a fresh interpretation of its meaning, develop new insights into its impact and re-tell it with a different 'spin'. The stories which emerged in the final version of *Past Times* are a considered and measured product; they have been subjected to a rigorous process of personal – and sometimes group – reflection, and every detail has been double-checked.

Reconstructing lives, and reclaiming individual and collective pasts, brought about a greater sense of self-esteem as group members increasingly came to see themselves as the holders of historical knowledge. This growing consciousness was further enhanced both by the group process itself, and the product of the group's work. In retrospect, it is evident that the process of remembering, and sharing memories, had proved hugely enjoyable to group members. However, it was the emerging and evolving product of the group's labours (*Past Times* in its various drafts) which transformed the group's dynamics and my own role.

The book has proved to be the source of individual achievement and collective pride. It inspired its contributors to go on with their own work. My original research aims became submerged into the group's own long-term and overriding aim: to keep working together to produce a 'bigger and better book' as documentary evidence of their own hidden history. The excitement generated by the appearance of the first draft of *Past Times* was captured in my diary entry of the time.

Extract 21

Tonight I was armed with 12 blue-covered copies of 'Past Times', which I handed out. I wanted to share this with everyone, as I thought they would enjoy finding out what we'd done so far. They couldn't read it for themselves, so I undertook to read it out loud. This went well. They were thrilled with the booklet. Brian asked several times: 'Can we keep it?'

They enjoyed listening and even Albert and Bert, who had said little themselves, enjoyed hearing other people's words.

Denzil kept putting his book on the table. Each time he did, a dismayed Brian said: 'No Denzil, it's all right, that's yours, you can keep it.' And each time, with a start, Denzil picked it up again. No one could read. But they opened their books at the right page (with help) and turned a page when I did. They sort of followed the story that way. It felt really nice. They were so pleased and proud.

The book, of course, was a wonderful trigger. It was compiled from their words, and their memories, and so it led to more and more memories. I got the opportunity to check out bits of people's stories which I had barely understood, e.g. Brian's game of 'Piggy'. New stories were told. Old stories were re-told and clarified. Sometimes the clarification led to verification from someone else; e.g. Brian's account of a hot plate wrapped in a blanket, to serve as a bed warmer, triggered an affirming response from Margaret. It was a super session. Everyone loved hearing their own words.

(Diary extract)

The diary entry was written after our sixteenth meeting. The process which started that night continued for the remaining 14 meetings of the group. Over a period of weeks I read the entire contents of the first draft of *Past Times* to the group. The readings took a long time because of the process I described; the booklet acted as very personalized trigger material to group members, and drew out more detailed accounts and further examples. The second and third drafts were produced in the same way, following the same sequence. This process could, almost certainly, have continued indefinitely, as each set of readings led to the revealing of more and more memories.

A key feature of this process was the emergence of shared memories of hospital life. Sometimes the mention, by one person, of specific names, or the recall of a particular incident, would spark off somebody else's memory of that time. Shared accounts also emerged, interestingly, even where people had lived in different hospitals, or at the same hospital but at different times. Some aspects of hospital life seemed to have almost a universal and timeless quality.

This next extract (Extract 22) illustrates the former point, and shows how Margaret and George's memories of the same hospital, and the same staff, coincided. (The names of the staff have been changed.)

64

Extract 22

Margaret:	After 20 years we changed over, and it was Sister Smith.
Dorothy:	Was she on the children's ward?
Margaret:	She was on F2. And then we had Moffat. She was on F1. She died in the end.
George:	She was a wicked old devil, she was! No wonder she died!
Margaret:	Old devil?
George:	Yes!
Margaret:	You're telling me! And Smith!

(Tape transcript, meeting 19)

Whilst the group format, where memories were exchanged and shared, led to a consensus view of institutional life, it was a consensus of a particular kind. In a very real sense, it served to sustain and justify the group's distinctive history, a history which hitherto had remained largely hidden or marginalized. The loss of home, family and freedom, which long-term hospitalization brought about, were remembered and felt keenly. Those memories were, of course, very personal ones. But the other memories of hospital days which were evoked in the group were characterized, at least in the telling, by defiance and humour.

I had set out initially in the group to focus on ordinary lives, to spare people from painful memories, and protect them from their own pasts. This was, of course, a misconceived – if not patronizing – mission on my part, although it was well-intended. I could not protect people from their pasts, nor should I have tried. Hospital stories, when they emerged, were certainly painful. But they were also tales of survival. And the very act of telling the story, to a supportive and sympathetic audience, was itself an act of survival and defiance. This was where a sense of collective hurt emerged, and this led to a collective denouncing of the causes of that hurt. There was solidarity in the group as they told their stories of hospital life.

Various stories were told, and I will look in detail at the content and meaning of some of these stories in a later chapter. Here I will just mention one enduring feature of hospital stories which struck me: the role reversal. This was a classic theme, whereby the patient became the 'hero', and the charge nurse, doctor, or superintendent was portrayed as the 'fool'. The following story is told by George (Extract 23). His co-conspirators are Albert and Bert, and the object of their attention on this occasion is Baxter (not his real name), the farm bailiff employed by Bromham Hospital.

Extract 23

George: Baxter was the farm bailiff when we were at Bromham, and he had a bike. Me and Bert, and old Albert, we used to get together and put it up the chimney. There used to be a, you know, those big chimney pots on top of those farmhouses. We had a big rope, and we tied old Baxter's bike on this rope and put it right up the chimney. And, of course, this certain afternoon Albert had done it. It was a Friday, and old Baxter comes out of his office and says: 'Goodnight you men, I'll see you on Monday, it's my weekend off'. 'Course, old Baxter couldn't find his bike, he didn't know where it was.

(Tape transcript, meeting 18)

This story, and many others, became part of the compilation of accounts now known as the book *Past Times*. Put together, the individual stories of group members carry a stronger message than stand-alone stories. They highlight and reinforce important period details and point up universal themes. At the same time the overall historical account is told through the individual voices of the group members. Every thought, idea and observation in the book is attributed to a person. The pride people felt in the product of our work together was two-fold. They were proud of their *personal* contribution, however modest, but they were also exceedingly proud of the document as a whole, both in terms of its overall size (it did get 'bigger') and the richness of its content (and 'better'). And so it was that, in time, their *collective* effort came to be valued too.

6 Narratives of ordinary lives

This is where I turn to the 'findings' of the research. They are also its product in the form of the book *Past Times*. It is in its final and polished version that the book represents the true voices of its contributors. They speak as individuals about their own lives, but in so doing they connect with the lives of others, both in the group itself and beyond it.

Many of the contributors' accounts of their childhood and schooldays are likely to resonate with other people's memories of the same time, or with the memories of their parents and grandparents. They also serve to mirror some of the visual imagery of the earlier years of this century as it has been recorded on film and in photographs. These memories of 'ordinary lives' will be the subject of this chapter.

There are other memories in *Past Times*, however, which most people probably cannot identify with, as they are outside their experience. I include in this many of the painful accounts of separation and rejection which occur in the book, but I also include the experience of being 'put away' in a long-stay hospital. The view, from the inside, of life in a long-stay hospital helps make *Past Times* a valuable historical document. The oral historians do not emerge in their accounts solely as victims of an oppressive system – which they were – but as people who survived, and often defied, the worst aspects of that system. These 'stories of segregated lives' are the subject of the next chapter.

One of my overall aims was, of course, to enable people to talk about the ordinary and everyday aspects of their lives. This was to avoid dwelling on differences throughout the project; instead, the points and landmarks in their lives which intersected with the lives of other people around them would be drawn out. As well as differences I was seeking commonalities. I wanted to collect some narratives of ordinary lives and, to some extent, I succeeded. They came in three sorts: deeply personal memories of family life; collected snippets of everyday life; and extended narratives of adult life. I will look at each of these in turn.

Personal memories of family life

I start here because this where group members started. They wanted to tell their stories in their own words about their lives, starting with their families. This meant revisiting their childhoods and, in particular, revisiting their families. These were deeply personal, often moving, accounts of family life as group members remembered it. There were some happy memories recounted but – where they existed at all – they were often couched in a context of current and later losses.

Remembering families meant remembering unhappy times – in spite of my safe topics policy. Some families were unhappy places for children to be. The accounts in this section are individual and personal; often they are stories of individual unhappiness and personal pain. But they are ordinary stories of family life for their place and time and so they belong here.

George, for example, remembers suffering as a child at the hands of his mother. He was the only surviving child as his brother was drowned. Later memories of life as a young man with his father were more positive, but the reference to suffering with his nerves at the end of this account was the precursor to his final departure from home into a long-stay hospital.

Extract 24

George: I didn't have a nice mother, I didn't like her. I think I was better off without her. She didn't like me, I don't know why. She used to hit me, knock me around. I was 12, I think, about 12, when my mother died.

I got on well with my dad. He worked at the brick yard at Stewartby about three and a half miles from Wilstead. He used to bike there and bike back. He used a cut-throat razor. He used to smoke a pipe.

We used to play dominoes, me and my father, in front of the fire. We used to start at half past six, quarter to seven, we used to play till about eleven, then we used to say, 'Shall we go for a pint? We'll go and get a pint', he says, 'they're still open'.

We had an organ at home. I believe it was given to us, it belonged to my father's father, my grandad. Dad didn't have time to play it. And he wasn't an organ man really, he was more of a drinking man. He used to like his pint.

I had one little brother, but he died when he was a baby. So I was the only one.

My grandad was getting on a bit. Of course I wasn't old enough to milk a cow. I went and got them from the field, took the old dog with me, got them in for milking. Ninety acres farm, he had. He had some hens, a few pigs. I used to collect eggs. I remember we used to make butter when I was at my grandad's. I used to help him make it when I was a little lad.

After school I suffered with my nerves so they thought I might be better off if I went to work and live with my uncle. I lived with my uncle and his wife on his small farm. I sometimes had to push their baby round the yard where it was   very   bumpy. Once I nearly tipped the baby out of its pushchair and my aunty was very rude. She said, 'You're hopeless round here! You'd better leave!' So I went back to live with my dad.

(Past Times, pp. 3-5)

George's family memories were mixed. He always spoke warmly about his father and enjoyed talking about the pubs and dominoes of his youth. By way of contrast, Edna's memories of her childhood were almost entirely unhappy. The family split up as a result of her father's drinking and violence, and she and the rest of the children were taken into care. She later returned home to live with her mother but lost her through death. Although she came from a large family, she had subsequently lost touch with everyone.

Extract 25

Edna: My mum worked in a chocolate factory, she used to bring us bits of chocolate home.

My father was no good, we was put away in a children's home. He was drinking every night, he hit my mum.

There were ten children, I was the youngest. My mum had ten, but four of 'em died. My father used to kick my mother when she was carrying you know. She lost 'em. I had three sisters, Doris, Hazel and Lily, and two brothers. I had three brothers but one died.

I wasn't at home when I was small, I was in a children's home in Luton. My brothers got put in Beech Hill, the boys' home. I was 14 when I came out.

My brothers were in the boys' home and I was in the girls' home. I was at Winston Girls' Home, at Farley Hill, and I went to a girls' school across the way. We used to have milk at dinner time, milk in the school playground. My sister was there, my sister used to be in the home with me.

Then when I was a certain age I came out, 'cos my brother came from abroad and he got a house. He used to go to London every weekend, courting, and then suddenly he got me mother this place in Luton, Farley Hill.

I used to do what I liked, my mum used to let me do what I liked when I was 14. She said, 'No discipline or nothing, you can go to bed when you like.'

My two brothers were in one room, my sister and me in another. My sister used to go up the wall, come home with no shoes. My brothers were in their bedroom, they kept tickling one another in the night. I could hear them.

Then me mum just went and died, suddenly. She got knocked down and died. She's been dead 11 years. So my brothers got married, and then we all separated. I don't see any of 'em. They don't come and see me while I'm in the flat.

(*Past Times*, pp. 5-6).

Edna's story is very much about loss and separation: the early loss of her family home, and to a great extent, the 'loss' of her childhood. There were later losses to cope with too, such as her mother's death and the fact that none of her remaining brothers or sisters have kept in touch. Margaret's childhood was difficult too, mostly because of the stormy relationship between her parents. The family did not split up, however, although Margaret herself was taken from the family as a child. This is not mentioned in the following extract, although other subsequent losses are included – the loss through death or separation of her two brothers and two sisters.

Extract 26

Margaret: My mum was terrible. She used to put my dad in punishment. She used to flirt with another man. He found out. He come home one day and she was shouting around, and he come in

70

and asked what was going on, asked her why she was shouting. She threw the dinner at him! Then he hit her! He hit her and then he walked out, went up the pub. Mum went up the pub then to see where he was. They had another argument up there and she come home. They patched it up, they made it up. He come home six hours after.

Sometimes she wouldn't talk to him. Sometimes she wouldn't talk to any of us! We couldn't do anything, we just put up with it. She might do it all day, sometimes several days. She was thoughtless.

I got on best with my oldest brother, Peter. It's his birthday on 17th November, he'll be about 72 now. I don't ever see him. [...] Two of the younger ones, Freda and Fred the twins, are dead, they both died a long time ago. Kathy lives in Manchester – Middleton, Manchester. I don't hear from her either.

(*Past Times*, pp. 6-7)

Margaret uses one incident to give a flavour of the tensions between her parents. Sometimes these led to arguments, sometimes to days of silence. Interestingly, in her retrospective and reflective account, Margaret uses the language of the hospital to describe what happened to her father when her mother was angry: 'She used to put my dad in punishment'. Ordinary memories, perhaps, but couched in the language of later less ordinary times in her life.

Brian's account of his family is similarly mixed, with happy and unhappy memories intermingled. Often he talked with relish about his family home in Yorkshire, but when he came to talk reflectively about his parents, his enthusiasm was tempered with some less than idyllic memories.

Extract 27

Brian: Mum was a bit moody, though sometimes she were all right. I could have anything I wanted! When she was in a bad mood she'd go off t' deep end!

One day I was doing something, I'm not sure what. She said, 'Don't do that!' I said, 'It's not my fault!' So she went off t' deep end. I said, 'But you told me to do it!' 'I know I did!' I started creating then, crying, and then, well, I made it up with my mum again. I told her I was sorry about what I did. She said, 'Come out of the way'. And she put it back in t' right

71

place. Oh dear, she were in a bad mood! And I were crying an' all.

Later on, when she were in a wheelchair, I used to push her around. I took her down to Shipley Glen, I took her to Bradford, I took her to Shipley and Keighley, I took her all over on t' train. We went shopping all over. Her leg was giving away at the back so she was in a wheelchair. She had the walking stick that I've got, that I were using for a while because my legs were bad. It's still in my bedroom, that walking stick, it's still there.

Dad was a little man, about as big as me. He were all right, my dad. I only saw him in one bad mood, when he was angry.

Dad used to work in a place where you kill sheep and that. Dad, me and my brother Malcolm used to go and sleep in this place which had rings on the floor. We used to take a torch to see our way down the street where they killed all the cows and that. It was dark, we used to go there when it was dark. It were an abattoir, and dad looked after it for somebody who got took poorly. My dad did it 'cos the other man couldn't do it. He was just there at night time. [...].

Dad and me used to go up to North Cliff. We'd take some sandwiches up there 'cos we had an allotment up there where we grew us own stuff. We grew all us vegetables and that. It's all big football fields now, but we had an allotment up there. We used to grow all sorts of things till one night all our tools got pinched, everything, we had a lot there.

They called my kid brother Malcolm. They called the younger one Albert. And I've got three sisters as well – Pamela, Marjorie and Dorothy. I think I'm the oldest, I'm not really sure. When we lived in Short Street my sister Dorothy wasn't born then. She never lived in our back-to-back house.

(*Past Times,* pp. 8-10)

In his account Brian talks about his family within the context of the times. He actually 'places' his parents, and siblings, in their back-to-back house, situates them geographically in West Yorkshire and adds in references to their allotment and his father's nights at the abattoir. Brian was unusual in the group in that he had never lived in a hospital.

There is not the space, nor is there the need, to include everyone's memories of their families. The four narrators, George, Edna, Margaret and Brian, between them demonstrated three important points. First, they showed that they – and, presumably, other people with learning disabilities – have the capacity to recall their lives, to reminisce about former times, including unhappy memories, and to recount their experiences to others. Second, they showed their willingness, and their ability, to act as witnesses of the past, to tell their stories against the backcloth of the times they were recalling. And, third, the family and childhood memories of these four people with learning disabilities were deeply personal, sometimes tragic. They were shared with others over time, as trust developed. Their 'ordinary' memories included rows, drinking, beatings, domestic violence, family break-up and – for one child – removal to a children's home. These events were not in themselves to do with anyone being labelled as having learning disabilities (the labels came later); these were the misfortunes of troubled families in bygone days. Later losses for George, Edna and Margaret were due to the change in their circumstances when they became long-stay patients and lost touch with their families.

Snippets of everyday life

My initial safe topics policy, and my later recourse to reminiscence aids, meant that I created many opportunities in the group for people to talk about aspects of ordinary everyday life. These were personal memories too, but they were often shared by others, and resonated with all of our memories of the time. Put together, these individual snippets of times gone by were able to build up a vivid picture of former times. They form a series of joint accounts – such as schooldays, home life, and street or village life – which recreate scenes from everyday rural and urban working class life in the early and middle years of this century.

Take schooldays, for example. Although some members of the group were sent away from home in childhood – to a hospital, children's home or boarding school – everyone still had their early memories of going to an ordinary local school. This was a popular theme to which everyone contributed. The extract below is taken from the 'School life' section of *Past Times*.

Extract 28

John: I walked to school.

Margaret: I used to walk to school. It was a good long walk, to Toddington, across the green, up to the top road. I walked along the green, up the hill, through the gate. We used to roll oranges down the hill.

Bert: I didn't stick school for long.

Albert: I didn't go at all.

Brian: I got the cane sometimes when I were late.

George: I didn't live very far away but many a time I used to be late! I used to do it on purpose. School started at 9 o'clock. Sometimes I wasn't there till quarter to ten! I got hit with the cane across my behind many a time for that. I used to shake 'em though. I used to put something in my trousers and I used to break the cane! I used to have some paper, or tin, so – it was a woman – she bent the stick!

I had a catapult. We used to play marbles. We used to flick cigarette cards, and some would land on others. It's called 'Flicksies'. You'd take it in turns. If your card landed on somebody else's, who went before you, you'd pick up theirs and they'd be yours. You'd just stand there and take a turn at flicking. Then someone else would have a go.

Brian: We used to pass comics right round – Dandy and Beano, Rupert Bear, Rocket. There was Black Bob as well, he was in a comic, a dog. The same one would go right round in a week.

John: We had milk in the morning break. We had milk monitors.

Margaret: I used to get two bottles of milk. I used to be one of her favourites. She used to say, 'Do you want another one Margaret?' and I'd say, 'Yeah, I'll have another one.'[...]

John: School dinners weren't very good. They were mushy, all mushy!

Edna: I used to go back to the Home for my dinner, then I used to go back to school after dinner. And then in the afternoon we used to have a pint of milk.

Margaret: When I was at the junior school, I used to leave school at 12 o'clock and take my dad's and the other farm workers' dinners.

(*Past Times*, pp. 11-13)

This is a short extract from a much longer account of remembered schooldays. Even in this relatively short account group members between them conjure up a picture of everyday life – of school dinners and milk

74

monitors, cigarette cards, catapults, comics and marbles. Some memories are very personal – Brian and George remember being caned; Edna remembers going to school from the children's home; and Margaret recalls how she used to take lunches out to the fields for her father and the other farm workers.

One of my very earliest safe topics was on the theme of home life – what sort of house people had lived in, what it was like, where it was situated, and so on. As I highlighted earlier, transporting people back in time to their earliest memories inevitably led to the disclosure of 'unsafe' and painful memories. Nevertheless, the theme did work to the extent that a joint account emerged which again recreated scenes from everyday life. The following extract from *Past Times* captures some of the group members' individual and shared memories of their home life.

Extract 29

George: I lived in an old-fashioned house, at the bottom of Wilstead Hill. It was all in one, a row of cottages. Where I used to live was just a village. Ours was a forest cottage. One up, one down. That's when my mother was dead. There was only me and my father then.

Brian: We had a back-to-back house with a cellar and gas lights. We had a coal fire and a coal hole!

            Once when we got locked out, we had to get in through the coal hole. That's when we lived at Short Street. We had to slide down the coal hole. We got really dirty.

Albert: We lived in a council house in Blunham. I helped dad in the garden.

            We had no bath at home. Elsie took me to have a bath at my brother's.

Bert: I know what I remember about our garden. I used to get apples off the tree. I had teeth then. [...]

George: We used to have lamps, oil lamps, and candles at home.

Edna: I fell down the stairs with my oil lamp, right from the top to the bottom. Someone said, 'It's a big fat elephant coming in!' I couldn't help it, I missed the stair. I didn't half hurt myself.

Margaret: We had candles not lights, 'cos you didn't have anything in those days. Not like the lights they've got now.

Edna: We used to have gas lights.

75

Brian: We had gas lights. In our back-to-back, down the cellar, there
              was a thing with two mantles on. Two mantles used to light
              up. It was gas. [...]

              When it was cold we had the fire on night time and day time.
              We used to black lead around the fire place an 'all to keep it
              nice and clean, shining. You used to get it all over your hands,
              you'd get covered in it.

                                              (*Past Times*, pp. 18-21)

This discussion continued and went on to cover baths, washdays and many
other features of everyday home life as group members remembered it. The
forest cottage, the back-to-back, and the council house all get a mention; so
too do gas lights and oil lamps, candles, cellars and coal fires. One of the
points I made earlier was that people with learning disabilities were rarely
listened to because it was felt they had little or nothing to say. And if they
spoke at all, their accounts were assumed to be partial and flawed. They were
thought incapable of expressing feelings, of thinking abstractly, or of being
reflective. They were not to be relied on in matters of detail; times, dates and
the chronological order of events were thought to be beyond them.

   And yet, here in the Past Times project were people with learning
disabilities who gave the lie to those assumptions. They could do all of those
things, given the time and opportunity to do so. They were good witnesses of
a past era. They brought back my own memories, but they also went further
than that in bringing back the stories I heard my parents tell about their past
lives. Like many older witnesses engaged in a process of reminiscence, group
members would pause occasionally to make a comparison between then and
now. In this extract it was Margaret who made the comparison, between the
candles of her childhood and the electric lights of today: 'Not like the lights
they've got now.'

Narratives of commonalities

My rationale for including the ordinary and the everyday aspects of people's
lives was to keep some sort of balance between competing, and
contradictory, forces. I hoped to strike a balance between the ordinariness of
people's lives and where they differed from ours – so that commonalities
between us would be as striking as the differences. I hoped to strike a balance
between people who are often seen, and represented, as victims but who
continue to see themselves as survivors. The autobiographies of people with
learning disabilities, whatever else they include, also feature the ordinary and

the everyday aspects of their lives; so I aimed for that balance between the labelled person and the fully-rounded human being who – given a chance – would emerge from people's own autobiographical accounts of their lives.

Some such accounts emerged, over time, a process which was encouraged to some extent by our small-group work. These were extended narratives about people's lives – where they were the active subject, acting and reacting, shaping their own lives, rather than forever being acted upon. They were narratives of commonalities, where group members told stories about getting into mischief and doing good turns as a child, and about holding down a job in adult life.

As these are relatively long accounts, I shall have to be selective in illustrating how they were used. As other extracts have focused on childhood memories, I propose here to look at group members' accounts of earning a living. Mostly they were excluded from the workforce, but there were times in their lives, before or after their long periods in hospital, when they were engaged in the world of work. As Brian was never hospitalized, he has several jobs to look back on.

Extract 30

Bert: After the war I was working up London, with my brother and dad, clearing the bomb sites. I was washing the walls and pulling the old paper off. This was on Saturdays and Sundays. I got sick while I was doing this and was in hospital for ten days. It was a very dirty job on the bomb sites.

Brian: Dad and me both worked in t' mill. I used to put bobbins on pegs. And there was a hook and a pipe, and you used to put all the bobbins in a tub. You used to weigh the bobbins on the weighing scales, then we'd put 'em into a big skep and put 'em over by t' winder for these ladies to wind off. We'd put one or two bobbins in their skep, they used the bobbins on their frames. [...]

George: I used to work on a farm at Wilstead years ago. We used to plough with horses. I walked along with the first horse, leading him, the other lad was behind the plough. [...]

Brian: When I left the mill, I worked in a foundry. It were very 'ot it were. There were sparks flying everywhere. You used to have a little trolley on wheels and it had a thing on it, and you used to put hot metal on it and wind it along with a wheel. You used to push it along on a thing with wheels. [...]

I got told off one day 'cos I trod on a man's mould. I got into trouble, I got sacked for it, sacked by the boss. But it were an accident.

Margaret: I left Bromham in 1974, November 19th, that's when I left. The staff come and told me, the sister of the ward. I went to live in the hostel. I went to work in Biggleswade on November 20th.

I was in a factory working on frames, tapestry frames, doing fancy work by hand. They sold 'em. I got paid at the end of the week. I left there in October, a year later, when I was 53. I retired when I was 53. I had fits. I've always had fits, even as a little girl at school. I haven't worked since. I retired. [...]

Brian: I went to work in a big house, a garden, with a chauffeur-gardener. This man who lived at the big house had a chauffeur-gardener and I was helping the chauffeur-gardener do the gardens.

Once we watched the Boat Race in this man's house, me and t' chauffeur. The old man let us watch it. They were nice people. And they had a housemaid as well, and a cook to cook all their meals. He were an old wool-buyer. He used to have a big mill. He was a retired wool-buyer.

They had tennis courts and I had to roll 'em out with a big roller. It's not there any more now, it's all houses on there now. I worked there till the old man died and they packed up then.[...]

I used to cut the lawn with a motor mower. It were a big one, it ran away with me nearly! It used to be really powerful. I had to walk quick with it.

I used to have a little wooden plough, a snow plough, with a handle on. I used to go up and down the footpaths pushing this little plough, keeping all the footpaths clear. It used to push snow to one side, it kept the footpath clear for the people. And we had to do the drive as well, so they could get the car up, and we had to shovel that by shovel. It were hard work! [...]

Edna: I couldn't stick a job, I was always in and out of work. I worked in a brewery. I worked in a milk place.

I was doing the bottles, drink bottles in the brewery washing 'em and putting 'em in a machine. Then I went to a milk place, a dairy, and I fell behind the back of a machine, with the bottles. 'Cos I had wellingtons on and I slipped. I had to give that job up when I had to go to Leavesden.

Brian: I used to work on a farm when I lived in Yorkshire. I remember hay making, using a horse and cart. It was a bumpy road and, one day, the cart and the hay, the whole lot, came over and the horse came with it! All t' lot tippled over, the wagon and all t' lot came over, and all fell over, and the hay was all over the floor. [...]

(*Past Times*, pp. 49-57)

These are scenes from ordinary working lives. They are well portrayed, giving the details of the work place, and the nature of the work. They range from ploughing and haymaking with horses; to gardening on the estate of a retired wool-buyer and mill owner; to clearing bomb sites; and to working in a brewery, a dairy, a factory, mill and foundry. These were the ordinary and unskilled jobs of the time.

Although the focus in the discussion was on the commonalities between group members' experiences of work, and the experiences of their contemporaries, nevertheless there are points at which even these narratives deviate from what might be considered 'ordinary'. Brian recalls how he was sacked from his foundry job for a minor incident. Margaret's job only lasted a year before she retired on the grounds of having epilepsy. And Edna describes how she was in and out of work, but finally lost her job in the dairy when she was admitted to Leavesden Hospital.

So even the narratives of commonalities also began to hint at the differences between the lives of group members and the lives of others. These differences were couched in the terminology of sickness, hospital admission, epileptic seizures and accidents – not in the terminology of learning disability (or its forebears). My attempts to focus on what was shared with, and similar to, other people's experiences could go so far but no further. The work was unskilled; jobs came and went; and for long periods of their lives group members were outside the workforce.

There were other silences in group members' accounts of their adult lives. The focus, above, was on work but there was no comparable focus on other typical markers of adulthood. There was no discussion of courtship or of getting married, and no mention of children. Just as group members were, by and large, on the margins of the workforce, so they were effectively excluded from married life and parenthood. The label saw to that – but just to make sure, long periods of incarceration in learning disability hospitals during their adult years was an effective bar. The stories which emanate from these years of exclusion will be the focus of the next chapter.

One of the striking things about the accounts of ordinary lives, as featured in this chapter, is the level of detail about time and place, and the degree of accuracy about how things were. In Brian's account of his jobs, in particular, the level of detail about 'bobbin ligging' in the mill, and the making of wedges for the flywheels in the foundry, was so great as to make them too long for inclusion here. Similarly, his accurate naming of the plants and shrubs in his garden job took him into an account also too long to be included here. But they are remarkable as grounded and lived experience, told simply from his memory. There is no doubt that he had been there; he had witnessed these events, and had had these experiences.

Overall, the level of detail and accuracy in these accounts, and the capacity of group members to portray scenes from the past, have shown again that people with learning disabilities do have stories to tell. Given the opportunity, they too can be oral historians; they can be witnesses of the past years of this century. Through their words, and their memories, it becomes possible to see people with learning disabilities 'as people reflecting and choosing, enacting rather than acted upon' (Atkinson and Williams, 1990, p. 8).

7 Stories of segregated lives

The last chapter focused on the commonalities between the lives of the people in the *Past Times* project and the lives of other people. There were many aspects of their lives which were ordinary for their class and generation. Their memories of everyday life in the early and middle years of this century were both personalized and well-grounded in period detail. Even in those seemingly ordinary accounts, however, there were silences and omissions, as group members' lives had, in fact, been far from ordinary. And there were hints in the stories which were told that life was ordinary only to a point. Where that point occurred in individual lives might vary, but the time came, sooner or later, when group members left the mainstream and entered a separate world.

Stories did not stop at that point. Far from it. Group members talked willingly, and at length, about their experiences in this separate and segregated world. The stories of leaving home, and losing touch with their families, are very personal accounts. They were part of the life review process which I discussed in Chapter 4. Day-to-day aspects of hospital life were recalled with evident distress by some members of the group, as they struggled to make sense of their lives. Some experiences, and memories, were shared, and some tales were told jointly or collectively – even if narrated by one person – in a spirit of defiance. This was another way of making sense of people's lives, but it was done together. The system, and its officials, became the targets of humour, criticism and anger. These feelings were easier to manage, for all of us, than the sense of personal desolation which sometimes surfaced when the laughter had died down.

These stories of segregated lives are the subject of this chapter. I want to look at three aspects of these stories: their silences and omissions; personal accounts of loss, separation and rejection; and tales of hospital life. I will take each aspect in turn.

Silences and omissions

The major silences occurred, of course, where group members' lives differed from what was typical for their age, gender and class. As I indicated in the last chapter, there was silence about courtship, getting married and parenthood. These events had not happened, indeed they had been prevented, and there were no stories to tell. Some of the 'ordinary life' stories in the last chapter also included incidents which marked people out as different; for example, the job changes and losses experienced by group members overall, and the lack of paid work for long periods of their lives.

Most of the ordinary life stories which were told in the group were about childhood. Often these were cheerful and lively exchanges, and many of them are included in *Past Times*. There were stories, too, which were not told but were hinted at. Childhood had its happy moments, but it also had its struggles. There are glimpses occasionally, when the curtain lifts for a moment, of just what those struggles might have been.

Take school days, for example, for it would not be surprising if a group of nine people with learning disabilities had at times struggled with their lessons. Some of those struggles were made explicit:

Extract 31

Brian: I found tables really hard to do.

John: We used to write with pencils. I couldn't do tables. They were a bit hard.

Margaret: The first thing I remember about going to school in Sundon village – when I was five – is doing sums and reading and writing. I had a lot of trouble with sums but I enjoyed doing fancy work. [...].

(*Past Times*, p. 14)

Other struggles were hinted at. Albert and Bert's cryptic comments about their schooldays suggest they were either absent through truancy or had been excluded from school completely (on the grounds, presumably, that they were 'ineducable'). Bert said: 'I didn't stick school for long. And Albert added: 'I didn't go at all' (*Past Times*, p. 14).

George lived a stone's throw from the village school yet he was often absent or late. Was there a story behind his apparently light-hearted disclosure?

Extract 32

George: I wasn't always there. I used to play truant when I went to school. I was never there! I used to go there Mondays, Tuesdays and Wednesdays, then probably the other two days I didn't use to go.

(Past Times, p. 15)

Was school difficult to cope with? Perhaps George was avoiding the humiliation which Brian did speak about. I quoted Brian earlier when he talked about having to wear a dunce's hat ''Cos I couldn't write' *(Past Times,* p. 16).

Lessons were tough, but so too were the playground and the street. Again, much of the talk about 'fun and games' was lighthearted, and there were many apparently happy memories of children at play. But sometimes there was more than a hint that even the fun-things in life entailed their own struggles. At one level this is not surprising. Many of our childhood memories include those things which we couldn't do very well, or at all. In that sense group members' experiences of childhood struggles would probably have been shared with those of other people – had they been talked about openly. Instead, they were just occasionally hinted at. Brian came closest to breaking the silence in his stories about marbles and skipping.

Extract 33

Brian: We used to have a fire hydrant in the street, and we used to play marbles on it. You had to roll it and try and get the marble on t' fire hydrant. And if you got it on you could pick the other marbles up. I was a little bit – not very – good at it. I'd lose those that I'd won. I kept losing 'em and winning 'em, I did. I lost 'em all! He took 'em all then, he got all of 'em. I had a big bag full, and a jar, and I lost 'em all. The jar were empty. He made me skint, he won me, I had to buy 'em back again.

(Past Times, p. 37)

What started as a general account about playing marbles turned into a story of how he lost to another boy. Was this a regular occurrence? Or a one-off incident? It could be either or both in this account, as Brian does not say. He does admit that he was 'not very' good. Perhaps skipping was a less threatening activity; at least, as Brian says, it involved playing with girls rather than boys:

Extract 34

Brian: I used to play with the girls, skipping with the girls. We used to skip in our street. We'd say:

'All in together, girls.
Nice fine weather, girls.
O-U-T spells out!'

And you used to run out of the rope.

(Past Times, p. 38)

Group members' memories of their childhood extended far and wide. They talked about their local park, the fair on the village green, Billy Smart's circus, holidays and Christmas at home. Much of Edna's childhood was spent in a children's home. She joined in the exchanges in the group, recalling the good times she had had – but usually with the rider that she had been in the children's home at the time. Was she putting on a brave face in these accounts? Or did she really have such a wonderful time? Is there a story behind the story which was told?

Extract 35

Edna: When I was in the children's home, I went on holiday every year. It was lovely. [...].

I went to Great Yarmouth with the children's home and I went to the seaside. I used to go to Clacton, Southend, everywhere. I used to go everywhere. And we used to have a holiday an' all. When we come home, we used to do the shoes and then we used to wash up. [...].

When I was in the children's home, I used to go to an American party, where Americans were. And we used to have a Father Christmas, then we used to have a box of money and all sorts of American chewing gum and everything. [...].

(Past Times, pp. 35-36)

Although Edna says the annual holiday was 'lovely', I thought there were hints that it was far from idyllic. The return home seemed to sum it up; this was, after all, an institutional holiday and the shoes still had to be cleaned and the washing up done. The Christmas party also seemed very much a group outing, where 'we' did everything as a group and there were no individualized presents. . . .

Separation and loss

As I have already indicated, my emphasis, especially in the early weeks – months even – of the group, was on the 'safe' topics of childhood and schooldays. There were, of course, no such safe topics. Talk of childhood, family life and schooldays could never be safe for people who had experienced major losses in their lives at such times. All the talk in the world about picnics, parks and fairgrounds could not keep at bay forever the real things that group members wanted to talk about. Their wish prevailed. As part of the process of life review, group members recalled and recounted what had happened to them, as children or as young people, which had cost them their homes and families.

These are the stories of separation and loss. There are several examples in *Past Times* and they are very individual and personal accounts. The events they describe occurred at different points in people's lives and for various reasons. Often the loss, whatever it was, proved to be the turning point which determined that, sooner or later, this person would be labelled as 'mentally defective', and would pursue a separate path through life.

George remembers how, as a young man, he was taken early one morning to Bromham Hospital. It was to change his life completely. His immediate losses were considerable. As well as his home and his father, his photographs and his cigarette card collection, he lost his girlfriend, Gwendoline, and never saw her again.

Extract 36

George: My mother died, then later on I went into hospital. I had bad nerves. I had St Vitus's dance. I'm better now. I was in Bromham Hospital, between Northampton and Bedford. Then we went to Hasells Hall. From there we went to Fairfield Hospital.

I was in Bromham 20 years. I went there in 1938, March 3rd.

I ain't got any photos. I had ever so many at home before I went to Bromham but, you know, I didn't have time because the people who came to fetch me came so bloomin' early in the morning. I wasn't ready to go!

When I was at home, of course, I only smoked tobacco. I hadn't many fag cards at home. My tin wasn't very big – I used to put them in a tin – and I said to my father, when I was going to Bromham, I said, 'I'll take them to Bromham with

85

me, I might get something for them'. But of course the person that took me to Bromham, he came early . . . .

I used to have a girl, a nice girl, Gwendoline. She lived not far from my mother and father, in one of the council houses. I lost her when I went away.

(Past Times, pp. 39-40)

George's life changed dramatically on 3rd March, 1938, a date he has remembered all his life. He had lived, until then, with his father in the village in which he was born. He has, therefore, a wealth of memories of the very different life which he had led before he went to hospital. Many of the stories of those former times are included in *Past Times*.

The lives of some of the other group members took a different course. Bill, Edna, and Margaret, for example, lost their homes and families as children. Bill's life changed when his mother died. He was ten years old, and he was sent to a residential school.

Extract 37

Bill: My mother died when I was ten, it was a shame. It was her chest. She was an old lady, getting on. We had a big family. I have three brothers and a sister, Nellie, but I don't worry about them. I lived at Kingsmead School. I got visited once a month. Dad was in the army, then he was a car park attendant. He used to come and see me once a month. I had to work hard. My sister Nellie came and told me when Dad died. I was at Kingsmead School then.

In 1934, I went to Cell Barnes. I was 14. I left Cell Barnes in 1954, then I went to Hasells Hall.

(Past Times, pp. 39-40)

Unfortunately for Bill, his father died during the time he was away at school. Not only did he lose his surviving parent, and his only visitor, he lost the possibility of ever returning home. He went instead to Cell Barnes, the first of several long-stay hospitals in which he spent much of his life. (Hasells Hall was an annexe of Bromham Hospital.) He lost touch with Nellie and his brothers from that point on, a loss that he still feels even though he says 'I don't worry about them'. In their oral history of 'The Park' colony, Potts and Fido remark on how often people who had lost touch with their families would say 'I'm not bothered about them' or 'I'm not worried about them'. They suggest this is a way of coping with a loss which actually does matter and *is* a worry (Potts and Fido, 1991).

Parts of Edna's story have been revealed in other contexts throughout the book. Here the strands are brought together into a more flowing, narrative account of the losses in her life which set in train her life of segregation.

Extract 38

Edna: My father was no good, we was put away in a children's home. He was drinking every night, he hit my mum.

I didn't see my father, I didn't even know him. I was taken from me mother when I was small, when I was a baby, 'cos me father couldn't support us and look after us. I went to a children's home, we all did.

I wasn't at home when I was small, I was in a children's home in Luton. My brothers got put in Beech Hill Home. I was 14 when I came out.

When I come out, I lived with my brother then my mum. Then she went out one night and she got knocked down by a car, so she had to go to hospital. She had cataracts on her eyes, and then she died. I see no more of her.

I've two brothers and three sisters. But I don't see any of them.

I had a boyfriend when I was 17. He was called John. He was tall and fair, and he was 18. I don't know what happened to him. I had to go into Leavesden and I lost touch.

I was in hospital for about 20 odd years. I came out when I was 40. I went in when I was 17. I was in a place in Luton, and the Court put me in hospital 'cos I done something wrong. I was in this place on High Town Road, and I was 17, and I'd done something wrong so I got sent to Leavesden.

(*Past Times* pp. 41-42)

Although in her adolescent years Edna had spells at home with her mother, and some of her family, her institutional career really started with the children's home. The hostel on High Town Road came later, followed by her compulsory admission to Leavesden Hospital.

Margaret's misfortunes started in childhood too. Severe injuries to her knee led to a two-year period of hospitalization from when she was only seven years old. A few years later she was pronounced 'backward' at her village school and the die was cast. Margaret began her own long period of segregated living.

Extract 39

Margaret: I was up in the garden, on the swing, when a boy come along
and hit me on the knee. He hit me with a pram axle, an old
thing with rods all the way round it. I fell off the swing with
my leg under me, and I broke all the bones in my knee. I was
in hospital, Leagrave Hospital, for two years.

I was in hospital for a long time with my leg. I was only 7.
Mum and dad come and see me. We had a party on my
birthday, on the ward. I was there till I was 10.

I was at school in the village till I was 14. I was glad to leave.
We had a high and mighty teacher who asked me why I
couldn't read and write. I told her I just couldn't do it. We also
had a School Inspector come round.

When I was a little girl I was put away. I was 14 and a half. I
went to Cell Barnes to live because they said I was backward.
My dad refused to sign the papers for me to go, but the police
came and said he would have to go to prison if he didn't. I
cried when I had to go with the Welfare Officer.

I went to Cell Barnes in 1936, when I was 14. I was there two
years and then I moved to Bromham. That was in May, 1938,
the 11th of May. I was at Bromham 36 years! When I first
went there, in 1938, I was on G1. I was there till 1974, and
then I went to the hostel and I've been there ever since. I like
it at the hostel.

(Past Times, pp. 42-43)

In other sections of *Past Times* Margaret's memories of school days included
seemingly happier accounts of whip 'n' top and rounders. And yet it becomes
apparent in this personal narrative that school days must have been quite
difficult for her. It seemed that no allowance was made for the loss of
schooling for a crucial two years, nor any remedial help offered. Instead a
'high and mighty' teacher berated her for not being able to read and write,
and she was declared 'backward'. This was followed by compulsory
admission to hospital – a date which, like George, she has never forgotten.
Margaret uses the classic expression of the time: she was 'put away'.

Two group members had never lived in long-stay hospitals. This applied to
Brian and Denzil who had lived with their families well into adult life.
Although their losses had come much later in their lives, nevertheless they
had also proved turning points in their fortunes. They had not led segregated

lives but had become users of separate services such as a day centre, hostel and group home.

Extract 40

Brian:	I've lost both my parents. Mother died six years ago. I still miss her. Dad died when we were still in Yorkshire, he's in the cemetery.
	My mum's not with me any more now. She died.
Denzil:	I lived at Pulloxhill in an old-fashioned house with my mum and dad. Then we lived in a flat at Flitwick. When my mum and dad died, I lost my home and moved into the hostel. I don't like it.
	We had a house then a flat once in Flitwick. Mum and dad died and I had to give it up. I wanted to stop there. I had to go to the hostel. I don't like it.

(Past Times, pp. 40-41)

The death of a parent is always a significant event in one's life. In the circumstances of a person with a learning disability, however, it is often doubly significant. There is not only the loss of the person to grieve over, but there is the loss of home and all that was once familiar to cope with. In his account, Denzil still regrets those losses. He had not wanted to move and he has never become reconciled to life in the hostel. The phrase 'I don't like it' is like a refrain in his story.

These are individual, and very personal, stories of the losses which group members had experienced in their lives. Major losses, such as the death of a parent, could bring in their wake major changes in life such as admission to a hospital or a hostel. Often such a loss proved to be a turning point in people's lives which determined that they would henceforward carry the label of 'mental defective' with all that that entailed. The loss of a parent, and the loss of the family home, were major events for people to cope with. But there were many more losses which followed in the wake of admission to a long-stay institution: the loss of freedom; the loss of many of life's opportunities – to learn, to work, to get married, to have children; and the loss of huge chunks of time (20 years, 36 years . . . .). There was often the loss of brothers and sisters too, and the feeling of rejection which went with this. And this is a feeling which has not gone away. It haunts Edna, just as it haunts Bill and Margaret, that although they have got brothers and sisters, none of them have kept in touch and no one comes to visit.

Tales of hospital life

What happened when group members entered the enclosed world of the hospital? We have looked at what they lost and left behind; what were their new lives like? There were many tales told of hospital life. Some memories were, inevitably, very personal and often painful. But others were shared stories, shared either in their telling (whereby various people chipped in with their contributions) or shared in their ownership (where one narrator told the story, but did so on behalf of other protagonists).

The book *Past Times* contains examples both of the personal, and the shared, stories of hospital life. I will start with the more personalized tales because these were told as part of the life review process. It was important, at least for some group members, to look back at their hospital lives and try to make sense of them. Sometimes those memories were painful, and often they did not 'make sense'. Margaret tried to review her life by telling us what had happened to her when she was 'put away', aged 14, in Cell Barnes institution.

Things started off, it seemed in retrospect, not too badly – but they got worse. . . . .

Extract 41

Margaret: At Cell Barnes, when I first got there, the sister spoke to me and said I would be all right. She was kind and gave me a cup of tea. The babies' ward was downstairs, the girls were upstairs and the boys were on the other side.

I was 14 and a half. I started work the next morning, sewing buttons on shirts and trousers, and repairing clothes till 4 o'clock. Then we went back to the ward and had a sit down. In the evenings we used to go to the Girl Guides and play games and have singsongs, which I enjoyed. We also played netball and had dances on Saturday nights when we wore our best clothes. We went to Church on Sundays.

I left there when I was 16, and then I went to Bromham Hospital near Bedford. I thought how big it was, and they were building a lot of new wards. I was on F1 and then I moved to F2. I ran away from there. The sister on the ward didn't like me and I didn't like her. I was there 20 years and I was always scrubbing. After 20 years we changed over. I went to F4 the children's ward, the babies' ward. We had a sister down there who I used to get on with.

Sister Smith was on F2. When I was in the stores one day, there was a lot of mats and Smith said I had to clean 'em all. So I threw 'em at her! And she fell over! She put me in punishment there. I ran away from F2. We hid in a haystack and got frost-bitten feet. I ran away with another girl and caught yellow jaundice.

The sister would keep on at me, saying my work wasn't done properly. She was being horrible. I'd scrubbed the ward and she said I had to do it over again. I said, 'Well I aren't going to do it over again!' I told the doctor. He come round and he wanted to know what I was doing on the stairs again. I said, 'I've been told I've got to do it again, it wasn't done properly'.

I planned it with the other girl, we planned it together. She was fed up. She was doing the dayroom and dining room, cleaning and polishing. Then I was put on it, as well as scrubbing. We planned to get into Bedford, walk across the fields.

We left at nighttime, round about 6 o'clock when it got dark. Dark like this. So we went off across the fields and on the road, then we got to Bedford. [...]

(Past Times, pp. 75-77)

As well as recalling particular incidents – throwing the mats at Sister Smith (not her real name); re-scrubbing an already well-scrubbed ward; and talking to the doctor on the stairs – Margaret's story ranges over many years of misery. This was not just an odd unhappy week in her life. This *was* her life. She was at Bromham for 36 years in all, but spent 20 years on a ward where she, and the all-powerful Sister Smith, did not get on. Margaret spent 20 years of her life scrubbing floors, a job which she hated. Each act of defiance on her part led to her being 'put in punishment', which meant yet more scrubbing.

It is hard to see how any of this can 'make sense' in terms of an individual life. But at least the story was told to a sympathetic, and supportive, audience who listened with respect and shared some of Margaret's sadness. And now that the story is written down, both in *Past Times* and here, it will be heard more widely, and other people beyond the group will know what an institutional regime, in all its harshness, really meant for the person who had to endure it.

As she explains, Margaret had looked for help with her plight. She had written a letter and had talked to the doctor. When all else failed, she ran away. It was winter time, and she and the other young woman had to sleep in a haystack. They were caught the next day, and were returned to Bromham Hospital by the police. The incident had good and bad consequences, as Margaret explains below; she left the dreaded F2 ward but suffered badly from frost bite.

Extract 42

Margaret: We was took back to Bromham. And then one of the staff, male staff, come and took us down F3s. A lot of patients down there, it's a low grade ward.

The nurses were all right except for one, a friend of that other one. She started when I got down there. I said, 'You needn't start on me!' I told one of the sisters on the ward when she come down and asked if I was all right. I said, 'No, she's been on to me'. That was the sister and she told her off, told her to leave me alone.

I was lying on the bed a long time, with my frost bite. I went back to F2 and another sister was on the ward then. I never ran away again.

(Past Times, p. 78)

Several of the tales of hospital life were shared in the telling, either through joint contributions, or through a narrator telling a shared story. Wartime in Bromham Hospital was a shared story on both counts. Some of it was compiled from shared memories of several people; and some of it was told by George, at some length, on behalf of – and with reference to – Bert and Albert.

The following extract from the wartime reminiscences in *Past Times* illustrates both the joint account, involving George, Margaret and John, and the longer stories which George was prompted to recount, which combined detail with action, and which related to shared memories.

Extract 43

George: They dropped a bomb and it fell somewhere near Bromham. It fell in a field.

Margaret: Yes, we see that, we see the bomb. It come over F1, and we was all in the cloakroom, and a board fell down, and we see this bomb go over the top. Well I see it. The board had come down from the window, so we put it up again.

92

John:	I remember it, it come down in the cornfield.
George:	In what was called Bogus Field.
Margaret:	One dropped in the ground, and one down the road. Nobody was hurt.
George:	War was declared at 11 o'clock on 3rd September 1939. I remember where I was, I was in Bromham.

George: I remember me and this other chap were at the shop. We used to go to this shop every Sunday morning, for a walk. He used to be a good old man, a good old boy. I used to let him have fags and baccy on a Sunday. We just got in there and we just got served, and the shopkeeper told us Hitler had declared war on England.

One of our planes came down in a field. A Spitfire. One of those single-engine planes. He tried to land but he couldn't. I think he'd been hit. We had a look at him but of course we couldn't get too near because he still had his bombs on. But I think he'd been hit 'cos there were holes in it.

When I was at Bromham, there used to be a bloke, he was the second – you know, not the boss, but next to the boss – and he said to me, he said, 'George', he said, 'we'd better move if we want to go on living much longer'. I said, 'We'll be all right, Ted'. He said, 'Can you hear them planes coming over?' 'Yeah', I said, 'they're British'. 'No, they're not, they're from Germany!' he said. Then we dived underneath somewhere, I forget where. Anyway about twenty minutes later he dropped a bloody land mine, right in the middle of Sherrington. Bloody bomb. 'Bang!' it went. Yeah, a land mine.

We didn't do too bad really in Bromham. We used to grow our own taters and that. We had some land girls there and had some fun with 'em! Do you remember that, Bert, when Baxter had a lot of land girls on the farm? There were about 12 or 14 of them weren't there? And two women to look after them.

(Past Times, pp. 60-61)

Several members of the group had spent the entire war in the confines of a long-stay hospital. This was an unusual setting, and yet the stories were told in that characteristically upbeat wartime spirit of many oral accounts of the time. In some ways their geographical isolation was of benefit as bombs in the locality were so rare as to merit special mention. The relative self-sufficiency of the institution was also helpful in providing home-grown food for its inmates, a point George makes in his reference to growing their own 'taters' on Bromham's farm. Wartime memories were still very clear, and the accounts capture several of the everyday facts of war: the blackout, the bombs, the fighter planes, the land girls.

The war brought changes to the regime at Bromham, albeit temporary ones. The stories of the time were of people's experiences of war within the confines of an institution. They were different from wartime memories from elsewhere, but a similar sort of togetherness emerged even there, at least in retrospect as people remembered many of the same events. The war actually brought relief from some of the more oppressive aspects of the regime. Some of Margaret's few relatively happy memories of Bromham date back to the war years when several of the wards were used for treating both military and civilian casualties.

Extract 44

Margaret: We had a lot of casualties in F3, wounded soldiers and people. I used to make cups of tea for them. I was useful.

The ladies and children were on F3, and the soldiers were on the other ward. We had nurses there. We had a lady there with no legs at all! She was bombed in London. And only one arm! Her other hand was paralysed. She couldn't eat by herself. I fed her with tea.

We had a party on our ward at the end of the war. We had a singsong. I sung. We decorated the ward up.

(*Past Times*, p. 62)

This was a rare interlude, for Margaret, when priorities in Bromham shifted sufficiently to bring a change in her circumstances. She became a helper on the wards, making cups of tea and helping care for patients – a welcome break from scrubbing ward floors. The ward party celebrated the end of the war. Ironically it marked the coming down of the curtain on Margaret's changed fortunes. The pre-war regime, with its old priorities, was reinstated and that feeling of being 'useful' was swept away. What Margaret did not know as she sang at the ward party was that she still had another 30 years or so of institutional life to go through.

I want to turn to those years in the next chapter, and look at the regime through the eyes of the people who had lived there. What do group members' stories tell us about the working of the institution? What, if anything, do they tell us about the history of learning disability?

8 An historical account

One of my research interests, at the outset of the project, was to look at the history of learning disability as seen, and experienced, by people at the receiving end of the changing policies and practices which have prevailed in this century. The nine people involved in the *Past Times* project were part of the twentieth century history of learning disability. Their lives had been shaped by the legislative framework of their time, and their fortunes, to a large extent, had been determined by prevailing policies and practices. They had *lived* this history – could they now shed light on it?

The answer to this question did not come at once; it emerged in the fullness of time. But when it did come, it came in the affirmative. It seemed that the nine people involved in the Past Times project could – and did – contribute to our understanding of history, and they did so in two ways. The first way was through their biographies, because it was through the shape of their lives, and the changes they had experienced, that the broad sweep of history could be charted. Their own lives actually mirrored the major changes of the century. These biographical accounts came, of course, through the personal revelations made by group members, especially when they were engaged in the process of life review. I will look, in the following section, at how biography is influenced by history.

Group members were also able to shed light on the *details* of past policy, provision and practice through their day-to-day experiences of the regimes in operation. Many such details emerged, of course, through very personal reminiscences about institutional life, but others were compiled jointly by group members casting their minds back together to times gone by. Later in the chapter I will look at some of the historical details which emerged in the group through the processes of personal and joint reminiscence. Wherever possible, I will match those accounts respectively with personal revelations from elsewhere, and with local, documented accounts of past institutions and regimes.

Biography and history

What has biography to do with history? Can the life of one person, or even the collected lives of nine people, shed light on the history of learning disability? The 'sociological imagination', according to C. Wright Mills (1957), allows us to explore the relationship between history and biography, and how they intersect with the wider society of their period. A more practical manifestation of this imaginative link has been through the research of Bertaux (1981), and others, in using biographies to explore aspects of social life.

Biographies can shed light on historical events, and they can illuminate trends in society. They can point up the common influences on people, as well as 'the idiosyncrasies of individual response and action' (Humphrey, 1993, p. 167). But, as Jan Walmsley has pointed out, 'There is no one typical career of people with learning difficulties' (1994, p. 180). There is no single biography in the Past Times project which is truly representative of all other lives in that period. Instead we have a set of individual – but linked – biographies which separately *and* together can begin to give us some insights into the impact of historical events on the people who experienced them.

The nine people in the project, between them, had experienced the swings to and fro between institutional and community care which have characterized the history of learning disability in this century. George, for example, was born in 1913, the year in which the Mental Deficiency Act became law and changed the lives of thousands of people – his own life included. Brian, on the other hand, was born 20 years later, in 1934, and was never institutionalized. He might well have been – many other people were – but he continued to live in the community. This was prompted by the wishes of his family, but these wishes were given a boost in the 1950s when 'community care' became more fashionable. His move to a group home in the 1990s reflects the recent workings of the 1990 National Health Service and Community Care Act.

The chart (Figure 8.1) is a summary of the biographical details of group members. It is not complete in every aspect, but there is sufficient information to show where, and how, the major historical changes of the century influenced, and changed, people's lives. Seven people were institutionalized, each of them for many years. They were admitted, and detained, under the terms of the 1913 Mental Deficiency Act, and its successor, the 1927 Mental Deficiency Act, and were discharged only years later when the major policy thrust was towards community care rather than institutional incarceration.

The switch to community care is shown indirectly in the biographies of Margaret, John and Edna, who were discharged from long-stay hospitals in the 1970s to live 'in the community'. It is also reflected in the lives of Denzil and Brian, both of which took a different course. Although it was their families who initially established the pattern of community living for their sons, the provision of occupation centres and, later, of adult training centres (as they were called) helped support this pattern. As their parents died, then residential accommodation was provided in the preferred community alternative of the time – and not as heretofore in a long-stay hospital. In Denzil's case, in the 1970s, this was in a hostel, and in Brian's case, in the 1990s, this was in a group home. The drive to community care came so late in the lives of George, Bill, Bert and Albert that they moved straight from hospital to a residential home for older people.

Name	Year Born	School	Hospital	Hostel/home
George	1913	Wilstead village school	1938, Bromham (25)	Residential home, 1980s
Bill	1920	1930, Kingsmead residential school (10)	1934, Cell Barnes (14) 1954 Hasells Hall (34)	Residential home, 1980s
Bert	1920	Not known	c1940s, Bromham	Residential home, 1980s
Margaret	1921	Sundon village school	1936, Cell Barnes (14) 1938, Bromham (16)	Hostel, 1974
Albert	1922	Not known	c1940s Bromham	Residential home, 1980s
John	1925	1933, Girton residential school (8)	1940, Bromham (15)	Hostel, c1970s
Denzil	1930	Not known	Lived with family	Hostel, c1970s
Edna	1932	1930s, Winston Girls' Home (0-14)	1949, Leavesden (17)	Hostel, c1970s
Brian	1934	Local school in Shipley, Yorkshire	Lived with family	Group home, 1990s

(Ages, where known, are given in brackets)

Figure 8.1   Biographical outlines

How, and why, had seven people been caught up in the widespread move in the first half of the century to institutional care? A glance at the chart suggests some possible explanations. Three people – Bill, John and Edna – had been separated from their families as children. They had been sent away to a residential school or 'put away' in a children's home. That separation was the beginning of a separate 'career' in institutions, and it was compounded, in Bill's case, by the death of his parents; in John's case, by the fact that his mother was a single parent; and, in Edna's case, by the break-up of her family and the death of her mother. Their institutional career was, it would seem, determined by a combination of factors in childhood. Thus, the loss, so early in their lives, of their home, family and parents, meant that Bill and John were swept along to the next institutional port of call when their schooldays ended. Edna's severely disrupted life with her family finally ended with a court order when, aged 17, she was removed to Leavesden Hospital and detained there for 20 years.

Margaret was 'put away' as a child of 14 into Cell Barnes Hospital because, in the language of the time, she was ascertained as 'backward' at school. The reasons for Bert and Albert's admission to hospital were never revealed, although they did hint at similar problems with their own school days – by his own admission, Bert rarely went to school, and Albert revealed that he never went. Perhaps they were regarded as 'backward' or even 'ineducable'. George was admitted to Bromham Hospital as a young man of 25 because he had St Vitus's dance. His years in the community prior to his admission to hospital were characterized, at least in the stories he told in the group, by village life, farm work, and pints-and-dominoes in the local pub with his father.

What historical events are reflected in these biographical details? The main points at which these lives intersect with national trends and provisions are in 1913 (the Mental Deficiency Act); the 1920s (the 1927 Mental Deficiency Act and the Wood Report, 1929); the 1970s and 1980s (the 1971 White Paper; the ordinary life movement, and normalization) and 1990 (the NHS and Community Care Act). The events prior to the 1950s mark the setting up, and maintenance, of a network of institutions, and set the seal on the incarceration of seven group members. The dates, and events, from the 1950s mark the gradual fall into disfavour, and the dismantling, of the institutions, and the move to community care – a trend which, sooner or later, changed the lives of all members of the Past Times project.

The 1913 Mental Deficiency Act was passed following a series of surveys, and investigations, into the prevalence of, and the appropriate provision for, the 'mentally deficient' members of the population. In 1904, the Royal Commission on the Care and Control of the Feeble-Minded was set up, and reported in 1908 in favour of segregated provision for 'mental defectives'. A vociferous, nationwide campaign for legislation which would enact a framework for the ascertainment, certification and detainment of mental defectives followed the report – a campaign led by the National Association for the Care of the Feeble-Minded, and the Eugenics Society.

The report, the campaign, and the legislation itself reflected the growing conviction in Edwardian Britain that the most effective way of dealing with mental defectives was by their permanent, even lifelong, incarceration in institutions (Jackson, 1996). Incarceration was seen as appropriate for mental defectives of all types, but it was seen as imperative that the so-called 'feeble-minded' or 'high-grade' defectives were detained because of their

98

alleged propensity for involvement in various social ills, including anti-social and criminal acts. Furthermore, it was argued at the time that their relative likeness and physical similarity to normal people meant that all too often they 'lurked in the general population, posing as normal' (Radford, 1991, p. 453). Without strict vigilance, therefore, they could easily escape notice and, without lifelong incarceration, they could readily 'transmit their condition to future generations' (Jackson, 1996, p. 161).

The 1913 Mental Deficiency Act obliged local authorities to set up Mental Deficiency Committees to provide institutional care, suitable supervision, and guardianship for people they had identified as mental defectives. This provided the framework in which people categorized as mentally deficient could be segregated for life. The 1913 Act defined four types of mental defectives: idiots, imbeciles, feeble-minded and moral imbeciles. A Board of Control was set up to oversee the workings of the local authorities and their committees. Henceforth, mental defectives were to be certified by two doctors, initially for one year and subsequently for five-year periods. The scene was set, according to Stainton (1991), for the rapid expansion of large institutional facilities.

The 1913 Act was passed in the year in which George was born, although its implementation was delayed because of the First World War. Nevertheless his life, and the lives of people born in the 1920s and 1930s, were transformed by this move towards lifelong segregation. In 1924, the Wood Committee was formed jointly between the Board of Education and the Board of Control to look at the education and care of mentally defective children. The committee surveyed the likely number of children to be certified as mental defectives, and highlighted an anticipated shortfall in suitable places. As well as refinements to the classification of mental defectives, and suggestions about their training, the committee recommended that 'colonies' (as they were then called) should provide for at least 460 people in order to achieve the required number of places, and to do so with some economies of scale.

Explicit links were made in the Wood Report between mental deficiency and other identified social problems of the time, thus highlighting the continuing strength of the eugenics fear which still prevailed in the 1920s (Stainton, 1992). Indeed, several members of the Eugenics Society served on the committee and its chief investigator, E. O. Lewis, was also a member of it. His investigation of the incidence of mental deficiency suggested an increase in the problem since the last survey in 1908, especially in relation to feeble-minded people. The report, in reflecting on his findings, suggested that:

[...] feeble-mindedness is more likely to occur among populations of a generally low mental and physical level than elsewhere, that is to say, in slum districts and in rural areas with a poor type of inhabitant, and that broadly speaking it is likely to be most prevalent in a certain limited group, which may be termed the sub-normal group, of the general population. The evidence is not conclusive but it does at least point to there being some relation between the slum problem and the problem of mental deficiency [...]

(Wood Report, 1929, p. 83)

The report made explicit links between mental deficiency and 'much physical inefficiency, chronic pauperism, recidivism' (p.83). Feeble-mindedness was on the increase, it was thought, because of the greater fertility of the socially 'unfit' and the hereditary nature of the condition. The 'hereditarian explanation' adopted by the report, together with its 'alarmist tone', reflected the eugenic fears of the time (Jones, 1986, p. 85).

The 1927 Mental Deficiency Act amended the 1913 Act, extending its provisions. Locally, Bromham House in Bedfordshire was opened in 1931 as a colony for the care of mental defectives. Six people from the Past Times group, out of seven, (Edna was admitted to Leavesden Hospital) lived much of their adult lives there on the basis of the lifelong incarceration envisaged by the Mental Deficiency Acts. The institutional building programme was replicated throughout the country in those local authorities which – like Bedfordshire – had not already complied with the earlier legislation, and the number of people detained in institutions grew steadily. In 1939, there were 46,054 people living in institutions, and this number continued to grow until it peaked in the mid-1960s at 64,600 (Korman and Glennerster, 1990). The institutions changed their name and status, though little else, in 1948 when the NHS came into being and took them over as hospitals. They remained for many more years as separate, segregated establishments far from the mainstream of everyday life.

However, changes began to occur from the middle of the century, albeit initially on a small scale. The National Council for Civil Liberties mounted what was to be the first major challenge to the 1913 Act. At its national conference in 1951 it decried the workings of the mental deficiency legislation on humanitarian grounds. The NCCL later published the pamphlet *50,000 Outside the Law*, which highlighted the abuse of many people's civil liberties, often in a arbitrary way, through their certification and detention as mental defectives. In 1954, a Royal Commission was appointed to look at the law and provisions for people 'suffering from mental illness or defect'.

The 1959 Mental Health Act reflected the concern in the Royal Commission, and in many other sectors of society, that institutionalization was an expensive, and inflexible, provision which could be misused. Consideration was to be given instead to encouraging, wherever possible, alternative provisions in the community. The 1959 Act was a landmark in the gradual shift in policy from institutional care to care in the community. It dissolved the Board of Control, and abolished the old classifications of idiot, imbecile, feeble-minded and moral defective, replacing them with 'subnormal' and 'severely subnormal'. Certification was no longer required in all cases, and many people could now live in hospitals on a voluntary basis.

Although the 1959 Act marked the beginning of a more wholesale move to community care, it failed to touch the lives of those group members already in institutional care. Their lives were changed only in the wake of other more influential precursors of community care. The 1971 White Paper, *Better Services for the Mentally Handicapped*, was one such beacon of enlightenment. It reflected the – by then – widespread concern about conditions in the long-stay hospitals. An influential book by Goffman (*Asylums*, 1968) had highlighted the oppressive nature of what he called 'total institutions'. At the same time, the long-stay learning disability hospitals were being rocked from within by a series of scandals, and inquiries (for example, Ely and Farleigh Hospitals) which revealed ill-treatment and abuse on a wide scale. The scene was nicely set for the appearance, in 1969, of Pauline Morris's book, *Put Away*, which further revealed the true conditions in the hospitals. There was no doubt that, by the end of the 1960s, institutional care was in urgent need of re-evaluation.

The 1971 White Paper argued for a more pronounced shift from institutional to community care and, wherever possible, for people with learning disabilities (or 'mentally handicapped' people, as they were then known) to live with their families, or at the very least in home-like settings in the community. Hostel care was favoured as an alternative to hospital care, and some local authority residential places were provided as a result of the White Paper's recommendations. This happened in Bedfordshire, as the changed fortunes of Margaret, John and Edna testify.

The shift from institutional care to community care was accelerated throughout the 1970s and 1980s by a series of reports and initiatives. In 1979, the Jay Report was published (the Report of the Committee of Enquiry into Mental Handicap Nursing and Care). It enshrined the rights and individuality of people with learning disabilities throughout its discussion and recommendation. The influential King's Fund document, *An Ordinary Life* (1980), set out the principles of 'ordinary living' for people with learning disabilities, and set in train the ordinary life movement. The principle of normalization was also highly influential in shaping services in the 1970s and 1980s. The dual move towards hospital closure, and community-based provisions, continued throughout the 1980s, culminating in the 1990 NHS and Community Care Act. The remaining group members still living in hospital were discharged in the 1980s to a residential home for older people.

Personal memories of hospital life

In the last section I used some brief biographical details to set individual lives against the broad backcloth of history. In this section I propose to make links of a different, and more detailed, kind. This time the historical events, and changing policies, will be seen through the eyes of one of the people who lived through them. Margaret's biography will help bring to life the policies and practices of the past. After all, she was there. She saw, witnessed and experienced the everyday workings of the regimes established and maintained by the mental deficiency legislation, and its framework of inspection and control.

Much of Margaret's story is already familiar from Chapter 7. Here I want to revisit it in terms of its historical context. Margaret was born in 1921, in Sundon, a village in Bedfordshire 'between Luton and Toddington'. She was the second oldest of five children. Family life had its difficulties, but Margaret could remember quite a few details of home and village life in the years prior to the start of her hospital career. Some of these memories are captured in the following scenes from her rural childhood.

Extract 45

My mum used to make her own butter when we lived in Sundon, where I was born. I used to help, I used to turn the handle.

We used to have a tin bath, used to sit in front of the fire. We sat in the bath, in front of the fire. We used our tin bath for washing clothes out. Mum used to do it, I used to help her. [...].

We used to have a grocer's shop and a butcher's shop in Sundon. I used to go to the butcher's. I used to know the fella' and I used to get meat cheap.

I used to go to the grocer's shop an' all, and get some potatoes, cabbage and carrots. [...].

There was a picture house down our street. That was in Gas Street, it was on the other side of the road. The Picture Palace it was called. We used to get in for tuppence! I used to like old pictures, Laurel and Hardy, old films. I used to go with my two sisters.

We used to have a fair on the village green. There'd be roundabouts and swings. [...].

(*Past Times*, pp. 22-24; 29-31; 34).

Margaret's childhood was marred initially by a severe knee injury which led to two years of treatment in Leagrave Hospital. She was, in her own words, later 'put away' in Cell Barnes, a mental deficiency institution, because she was deemed to be 'backward'. This was in 1938, and she was aged 14. Although she remembers how she cried when the Welfare Officer took her away, Cell Barnes was, in retrospect, a relative haven compared with what was to come later. Margaret was there two years. Her first impression was a good one as she recalls:

At Cell Barnes, when I first got there, the sister spoke to me and said I would be all right. She was kind and gave me a cup of tea. The babies' ward was downstairs, the girls were upstairs and the boys were on the other side.

(*Past Times*, p. 75, already quoted in Chapter 7)

Margaret's description of the layout of the institution – 'the boys were on the other side' – makes clear that the strict segregation of the sexes, reported by people in institutions elsewhere, was operational in Cell Barnes in the 1930s. (See also, for example, Potts and Fido, 1991; Cooper, 1997.) Documentary sources also confirm the physical separation of boys and girls, men and women, in mental deficiency institutions. (See, for example, Stevens, 1997; Jackson, 1997; Atkinson and Walmsley, 1995.) School lessons were, it seemed, already a thing of the past, because on the very next day Margaret was set to work:

I was 14 and a half. I started work the next morning, sewing buttons on shirts and trousers, and repairing clothes till 4 o'clock. Then we went back to the ward and had a sit-down. In the evenings we used to go to the Girl Guides and play games and have singsongs, which I enjoyed. We also played netball and had dances on Saturday nights when we wore our best clothes. We went to Church on Sundays.

(*Past Times*, p. 75, already quoted in Chapter 7)

Again, these details of everyday life are confirmed by reports from elsewhere. Institutions were meant to be as self-sufficient as possible, and

103

clothes were made and repaired on site mostly by inmates. Sports, particularly team games, were characteristic of the time, as were troops of Boy Scouts and Girl Guides in mental deficiency institutions in the 1930s (Stevens, 1995). The Saturday night dances, and Church on Sundays, are also well documented as regular features of institutional life (see, for example, Potts and Fido, 1991).

Margaret was moved, at the age of 16, to Bromham House. Her first impression was 'how big it was', and how they seemed to be building a lot of new wards. This was 1938 and, it was true, Bromham was going through a period of rapid expansion. There were no Girl Guides, netball team or singsongs mentioned in this account. The emphasis was on work and punishment. As we saw in the last chapter, Margaret spent 20 years on one ward, F2, where she did not get on with the sister. Her job was scrubbing the wards – which she hated – and her punishment for any sign of reluctance or rebellion was to be given more scrubbing to do. Margaret's account reflects the first hand experiences of people in other institutions where a strict regime of work operated, and where punishments, such as extra scrubbing duties, solitary confinement and loss of privileges were everyday occurrences. (See, for example, Potts and Fido, 1991; Atkinson and Williams, 1990; Cooper, 1997.) The emphasis on work, and the drive towards the self-sufficiency and cost-effectiveness of colonies, is also confirmed in accounts based on documentary sources. (See, for example, Thomson, 1992; Radford, 1991; Atkinson and Walmsley, 1995; Stevens, 1997; Jackson, 1997.)

It was not surprising that Margaret ran away. Nor was she alone in her attempt to escape. George Mustard, for example, in Prudhoe Hospital in Northumberland recalled: 'Lots of us used to always run away' (Atkinson and Williams, 1990, p. 104). People ran away to escape the awfulness of their fate. The irony was, of course, that it was worse on their return because running away was a punishable offence. Margaret suffered frost bite, a spell in the 'low grade' ward and a return to the dreaded F2. Similarly, Mabel Cooper, in St Lawrence's Hospital, Caterham, talked about people who ran away and who, when they were caught, were locked up in G3, the punishment ward: 'They used to make you wear your bed slippers and then you couldn't run away' (Cooper, 1997).

Margaret tried to run away from the day-to-day unhappiness of her life. In the end there was no escape, but it was worth a try. The regime in the 1930s and 1940s was unremittingly grim, as she recalled with much sadness:

Extract 46

I lived on a miserable ward. It wasn't much fun, especially F2. There was always rows on there, rows with the staff. And the staff shouting around telling the patients to shut up. I didn't get shouted at ' cos I used to keep quiet. I was on F2 a long time, about 20 years.

(Past Times, pp. 62-63)

There was much personal animosity between Margaret and one of the ward sisters, a point she returned to several times by way of explaining the depth of her misery. She was, of course, an easy target for someone else's vindictiveness. There was little Margaret could do. She was virtually powerless, as to speak out invited denial and disbelief, and would almost certainly lead to more trouble behind closed doors. The animosity mostly meant that she spent her life scrubbing: 'One of 'em didn't like me, so I used to do a lot of scrubbing. I was on scrubbing at Bromham' *(Past Times*, p. 64).

However, there were other consequences of this vendetta for Margaret. She was very fond of her father. When she described her parents, she was critical of her mother, but spoke warmly about her dad – and with some sympathy for his plight. She recalled how he had initially refused to sign the papers which sent her to Cell Barnes, and had only done so when threatened with prison. He died while she was in Bromham. She was then aged 25, and his death was a terrible blow. Not only that, but she was not allowed to go to the funeral by order of that same ward sister on F2. She simply said 'no' and there was nothing Margaret could do about it:

Extract 47

Dad went in 1944. He died in 1944. He was 53. They didn't tell me why he died. My brother, Peter, wouldn't tell me either. He come to Bromham, he was in the army then. He told me dad had died. I cried, upset myself, I couldn't eat no food for a couple of weeks. They wouldn't let me go to the funeral, 'cos I was in the wrong. I was on F2 and the Irish nurse, sister, wouldn't let me go.

(Past Times, pp. 43-44)

This was a very real loss for Margaret but it was also, I think, a symbolic loss. The one person who might have fought to get her out of the institution was now gone. The rest of the family kept in touch and Margaret talked about their occasional visits. When her mother died, many years later, she opted not to go to her funeral. Now all visits have ceased:

Extract 48

Freda, my sister, come to see me once, one August, in Peter's sidecar. He had his motorbike then. And then he had a job getting her out because she wasn't well. So she stayed in the sidecar and I had to go out and see her. She died.

Mum died in 1968, she was about 85. Peter told me. He come and see me. I didn't go to the funeral, I didn't want to. She used to come and see me in Bromham. She came on the bus once, then Peter used to bring her in his car. Peter's got a car now, my brother. He used to come and see me in Bromham, but now he don't come at all.

(Past Times, p. 44)

Just as Margaret remembers the date she first arrived at Bromham, so she remembers the date she left: 'I left Bromham in 1974, November 19th, that's when I left. The staff come and told me, the sister of the ward. I went to live in the hostel' (*Past Times*, p. 53).

The swing away from institutional care towards care in the community had finally touched Margaret's life. A hostel had opened in Dunstable and 38 years after she had first left 'the community', Margaret returned to it.

Shared memories of hospital life

Margaret's life demonstrated the main shifts in policy over the years and, in the detail of her own story, she revealed the workings of the regime as she saw and experienced it. But no one life can truly represent all other lives and experiences, so I want to turn now to the shared memories in the group. What emerged from the joint reminiscence sessions? And how do these oral accounts fit with the documented history of the institutions in question?

Perhaps the best place to start is with names and dates. Everyone in the group was very clear about where they were sent, and most people knew when this was (including George and Margaret who knew the exact date). In 1938, both George (from his home) and Margaret (from Cell Barnes) were taken to Bromham House. What was this place like? And was it coincidence that two of my group members should find themselves taken there in the same year?

Bromham House was originally 'a delightful residence built for the late Mr W.H. Allen at the close of the last century' (Bedford Hospitals, 1960). The house, together with its outbuildings and 135 acres of land, were purchased in 1930 by the newly constituted Bedfordshire and Northamptonshire Joint

Board for Mental Deficiency. In 1931, the Board of Control licensed Bromham House as a Certified Institution for the reception of '12 high grade employable male defectives' over the age of 16 (Mental Deficiency Committee minutes). The very first inmates were admitted on 16th July, 1931. Their summer timetable was as follows:

6.30am	Rise
8 am	Breakfast
1 pm	Dinner
5.30pm	Tea
9 pm	Bed

(MDC Minutes, 11-5-31)

In 1932, the accommodation was expanded to take '12 additional high grade male defectives', and plans to house 60 adults were approved. A scheme for a colony of 260 patients received the approval of the Board of Control in 1936, and the foundation stone for the first villa was laid in 1936. The first Medical Superintendent, Dr R. G. Blake Marsh, was appointed in 1937, and in 1938 Sir Laurence Brock, chairman of the Board of Control, officially opened Bromham House Colony. This was the year in which both George and Margaret were admitted. They were part of a first wave of new admissions as the institution expanded to house 194 people.

The war broke out the following year and, like many other institutions at the time, some of Bromham's wards were adapted as an emergency hospital. The wartime memories of the group were highlighted earlier in the book, and they included Margaret's account of helping to nurse sick patients on the wards. Initially Bromham was used to look after chronically sick patients evacuated from London hospitals, but later it was also used to nurse military and civilian casualties. Two villas were used to provide 120 beds as part of the Emergency Hospital Service. It reverted to its original colony status after the war, and continued to expand. When the NHS came into being in 1948, Bromham had 280 patients on its register, 147 male and 133 female. The word 'colony' was dropped in 1950, when the title Bromham Hospital was officially adopted.

As well as Bromham House, group members also talked about other institutions. These included out-of-county mental deficiency institutions – later hospitals – such as Cell Barnes and Leavesden in Hertfordshire, but also included two other Bedfordshire institutions. These were Hasells Hall and Fairfield Hospital. They were talked about by George, Bill, Bert and Albert, each of whom pursued a very similar institutional career. They all lived at Bromham for long periods, but this was interspersed with a spell at Hasells Hall. In fact, Bill was admitted directly to Hasells Hall from Cell Barnes but later returned to Bromham to live. When they left Bromham, the four men moved on in their later years to Fairfield Hospital, a psychiatric hospital which had one ward set aside for people with learning disabilities. As they grew older, they swapped the ward at Fairfield for a special wing in a residential home for elderly people.

What was Hasells Hall? I had never heard of it before the Past Times project. I had, of course, heard of Bromham but somehow Hasells Hall seemed to have disappeared from local awareness – except for the memories of the people who had lived there. There were also references to it, as I discovered, in some local documents, but when group members – in our very first meeting – talked about Hasells Hall, I and the staff looked quite blank. They tried to explain:

Extract 49

Bill: Hasells Hall, 1964, Squire Pym.

George: That chap on the government it was his grandad's house. His granddad was Squire Pym. I don't think I'd recognize it now. They tell me it's all built up now, all flats round there now, at the top, in the hall where we used to live.

(Tape transcript, meeting 1)

The *Bedford Group of Hospitals* survey (1960) reveals that Hasells Hall, near Sandy, was acquired in 1950 as an interim measure to meet 'the growing need for more hospital accommodation in the region for mentally defective patients' (1960, p.86). The long-term plan, although it was never implemented, was for Bromham Hospital to expand to 1,000 beds. As an intermediate step towards dealing with the local waiting list, Hasells Hall was opened for the reception of 60 male patients on 21st September, 1953. They included four members of the Past Times group.

Hasells Hall was built in the 17th century. It had been improved and enlarged in the 18th century, and was 'for 200 years the seat of the Pym family who have been prominent in Bedfordshire affairs' (Bedford Hospitals, 1960, p. 91). The hall stood in 12 acres of land, and in 1953 it opened as an annexe to Bromham Hospital. The grounds included kitchen gardens which were to be cultivated by patients 'for the benefit of the hospital'.

A more glowing account of Hasells Hall appeared in the Luton Society for Parents of Backward Children Year Book, 1968: 'Hasells Hall is a large Italian-style mansion standing in a lovely wooded park of about 140 acres. [...] It stands on a high plateau and the views over the countryside to the west are very fine – from the roof of the Hall three counties can be seen. In the Spring, daffodils are everywhere and bluebells, too, are all over the woods.

The rhododendrons make a lovely show later in the year. The gardens and kitchen gardens are well-stocked and tended' (Year Book, 1968, p. 61).

But what about Hasells Hall as an annexe of Bromham? Again, the Year Book author writes positively about the regime, and the men who lived there: 'There are 70 men there now and there will probably be up to 100 before long. It is a very happy place due in no small part to the kindness of the Luton Society. Many of the men are well-known in Sandy. They come down to football matches, to cricket and all the garden fetes. Often, they go to Biggleswade and sometimes to Bedford. It is a really friendly place' (1968, p. 63). Would group members recognize this description? And would they agree with it? We shall see, below, more of what they thought.

Although Bromham and Hasells Hall were much talked about in the group, by way of contrast, Fairfield Hospital was rarely mentioned. George and Bill both acknowledged that they had eventually moved on to Fairfield. And Bert and Albert evidently did:

Extract 50

Bert: In Fairfield I helped stoke the boilers. That was a warm job, it made me sweat.

Albert: [...] When I went to Fairfield I helped get the coke in for the boiler.

(Past Times, p. 72)

But there was little else said. What happened there remains a mystery, even though Fairfield represents many years of their lives. Their progression from Hasells Hall to Fairfield Hospital was noted in the Luton Society for Mentally Handicapped Children Year Book entry:

> The mini-bus is always being used to ferry youngsters to and from the nursery and to visit the older mentally handicapped, now being cared for at Fairfields Hospital, but who were at one time at Hassels (*sic*) Hall.

(Year Book, 1970)

I want to return now to the shared memories in the group. One of the recurring themes was work. In the old days every able-bodied person was expected to put in a full day's work. This was organized according to gender. At Cell Barnes, Margaret had worked 'in the sewing room, sewing buttons on shirts' and 'at Bromham I was always scrubbing'. Meanwhile, at Leavesden Hospital, Edna 'used to polish and work over at the nurses' home' and, later, worked at the Industrial Training Unit for ten years.

The men were engaged in different work, much of it out of doors in the gardens and on the hospital farm. Bill's working life, at Cell Barnes, started –

like Margaret's – as soon as he arrived, aged 14: 'I used to do gardening. I used to work in wellingtons. Pea picking and potato picking'. John used to work on the gardens at Bromham.

Extract 51

John: Big gardens they were, at Bromham, a lot of people worked there. I didn't like pulling the weeds out, it was a dirty job. We grew plants; flowers and vegetables. We had a big greenhouse. We used to take flowers round the wards every Monday, and bring the old ones back.

(*Past Times*, p. 72)

Albert worked in the gardens at Hasells Hall. Bill, when he moved there, worked in the woodshed, sawing wood. At Bromham Bert 'used to chop wood for sticks for the fire. When I'd got enough I put them in bundles and tied them up with wire'. He also worked on the wards: 'I used to help the nurses bath the patients and sweep up the wards'.

There were many memories of farming, both at Bromham and at Hasells Hall, as these shared memories in Extract 52 illustrate. (Staff names, here and elsewhere, have been changed.)

Extract 52

George: We used to have pigs and everything there, and cows. You know, they still kept some pigs but had to part with the cows. We had a lot of pigs, I can't remember just how many, but we had about 40 or 50 pigs. That's a lot of pigs.

Albert: I did digging. Potatoes. And harrowing.

Bill: I used to work on a farm, for Fred Gilmore.

George: Yes, we used to work for a man called Mr Gilmore, Fred Gilmore. Him and another man, what was known as Wilf Carpenter.

Bill: He had a son called Eric Gilmore, and two daughters.

           The cows were milked by machines in a milking shed. I used to do this work with Fred Gilmore, when I was at Hasells Hall.

           We used to go to this farm halfway to Potton. They used to grow sugar beet, parsnips and lettuce. His wife came from Potton.

George: When I was there, I used to help with the cows and pigs. I had to clean 'em out and feed 'em, fetch clean straw and that.

(Past Times, p. 66)

And the reward for all this work? It was sixpence a week, or its equivalent in cigarettes or chocolates, as George and Margaret explained:

Extract 53

George: They used to give us 15 Woodbines a week at Bromham, that was all we had. They were worth sixpence [2½p]. They were tuppence a packet, and you got five in a packet. The people what didn't smoke had six pennyworth of sweets. That's all we used to get in them days. Them that didn't smoke had sweets, and them that smoked had fags. I used to get three packets, 15 for sixpence.

Margaret: You could have 5 Woodbines and a packet of sweets, but I never smoked. I just had sweets.

(Past Times, pp. 72-73)

These accounts are historically accurate in all respects. In her own research into local history, Jan Walmsley unearthed a report by the Board of Control inspectors to the effect that, in 1943, 87 per cent of the inmates at Bromham were 'employed'. Their work was 'gender specific' (Walmsley, 1994, p. 120). Men worked on the farm, in the gardens, or on the wards, or some were engaged in trades such as mat making and cobbling. Women were ward maids or domestics, or else they worked in the sewing room, kitchen or laundry.

The importance of the hospital farm was noted in the Bedford Hospitals survey: 'Farming activities played an important part in the communal life of the male patients, many of whom had come from the rural areas of Bedfordshire and Northamptonshire' (1960, p. 84). The farm was later discontinued. This was a change in policy nationally, following a directive in 1955 from the Ministry of Health. Just as George had recalled, the cows went first, then the pigs: 'Accordingly the dairy herd of pedigree shorthorns was sold and 60 acres of land acquired in 1950 let for grazing. [...] The farm machinery was sold and later the stock of pigs' (Bedford Hospitals, 1960, p. 87).

The payment of sixpence per week, or its equivalent, to patients for their work was referred to as a 'reward' in the Mental Deficiency Committee minutes of 14th December, 1931. The amount payable should be 'a maximum of sixpence per week'. The same amount was also paid at other institutions.

At Meanwood Park, in Leeds, for example, Douglas Spencer noted: 'Patients received six old pence per week or a bar of chocolate' (1990, p. 3).

The group members were good oral historians. They combined factual detail with biographical detail. They described their personal experiences, but they also shared many of their memories. What emerged was a fascinating mix of personal, biographical and historical detail, much of it verifiable from oral and documented sources, both locally and nationally. The auto/biographical approach worked in the Past Times project, so clearly it can work elsewhere. And much more work still remains to be done. The uncovering and recovering of the history of learning disability by and with people with learning disabilities, on a scale larger than mine, remains a challenge for historians and researchers both now and in the future.

9 Meanings and messages

In earlier chapters I have looked at many of the *Past Times* accounts in terms of their literal meaning: what they have meant personally, collectively and historically to the group members who separately, or together, contributed to them. Now I want to turn to a different set of meanings and messages, those that are less literal and conscious, and which could be seen and interpreted in more symbolic (even mythical) terms.

One of the traditions in the group, established from its very beginning, was the art of story-telling. This was story-telling as narration: the narrating of a bounded event, or episode(s) which involved characters and action, and which included the narrator as both actor *and* observer. Such stories could include, for example, the re-telling of a dramatic incident or the re-visiting of characters from the past. Where they differed from other accounts was in their function in the group, and in the messages they conveyed. These were no mere recounting of memories, and descriptions of period details, they were a way of conveying other meanings.

I want to look, here, at both aspects of story-telling: the act, and indeed art, of story-telling in the group; and the nature and content of the stories. Finally, I aim to explore the role and purpose of these stories in the group and beyond. What were they – myths or truth? And what (who) were they *for*?

The art of story-telling

The most noticeable feature of the story-telling tradition in the Past Times project was that it was a male prerogative. Not only that, but it was, more or less, confined to two men, Brian and George. This was in marked contrast with everything else which happened in the group where there was a universal quality to the act of remembering personal and period details of the

113

past. Story-telling was different. It had a different purpose, it had other meanings – and it was for men.

Gender differences in the telling of life-stories have been noted elsewhere. Women, it is suggested, often speak as 'we' to reflect their relationships and their membership of families and groups. In their recounting of their lives, women tend to reflect on who they are, in terms of their social self and their role in relation to others (Minister, 1991; Chanfrault-Duchet, 1991). Men, on the other hand, traditionally talk about themselves as the active 'I' and present themselves as decision-makers in their own lives (Samuel and Thompson, 1990). Men's stories tend to reflect their roles and tasks in life and what they did to achieve them. Men typically see their lives as their own, as a series of self-conscious acts with well-defined goals (Thompson, 1988). These gender differences were noted also in the anthology 'Know Me As I Am', where the life-stories of women and men with learning disabilities were seen to match this seemingly universal pattern: 'We found that women's stories involved the relationships that mattered to the author, but men's stories often focused more on a chronological account of life events' (Atkinson and Williams, 1990, p. 243).

There were, of course, only two women in the Past Times project. They certainly had stories to tell, many of which have already been featured in this book. They were, on the whole, of a very intense and personal kind: Edna and Margaret both talked about being 'put away' as children (no one else used this phrase although it was in widespread use in the past); they talked about their families, and the loss of them; and Margaret talked about the people she encountered, the good and the bad, in her many years in hospital. These accounts could be seen, at least in part, as relationships-based. Although they do tell other, more active stories, such as Margaret's account of running away from hospital, and Edna's mixed experiences of employment, neither of them used the distinctively story-telling mode used – and perfected – by George and Brian. Edna and Margaret wanted to tell it 'how it was'; to convey what had happened to them, and what it had meant. When it came to the art of story-telling, that was only part of what George and Brian intended.

Stories were told in a group setting. They had an audience and, inevitably, there was an audience-effect. Listeners could often identify with the story being told, and would listen with empathy and understanding. The stories of an intensely personal kind were often listened to in sympathetic and respectful silence. But some stories were shared with their listeners and, in George's case, often included his listeners. They were often told against a backdrop of audience participation, of a greater or lesser degree. This was story-telling, or narration, as a performance, a public display of narrating skills to impress or influence others (Finnegan, 1992).

Story-telling in the Past Times group was one way of holding the floor. So long as the narrator could keep going on his story, he had, more or less, the attention of other group members and at least temporary control of the group's direction. George and Brian told stories and held the floor in this way. In so doing, they were making a bid for the leadership of the group. They were my rivals – and they were each other's rivals. They vied with me, and they vied with each other. Their stories were not told to a group listening in respectful silence. They *took* time; they were not necessarily given it. They had each other to contend with, as well as myself and staff; and they often spoke against the background noise of listener participation. None of this daunted them, however, and their story-telling skills, if anything, got better through their many public performances.

In Extract 54, below, taken from the transcription of the sixteenth meeting, those skills and the George-Brian rivalry are well displayed. Two stories are on offer to the group, on two different themes, and they cut across each other.

Extract 54

George: Dorothy, if you don't mind, if you'll let me have a word in. [He smiles.] I remember at Bromham, I said to John one morning, I don't know if John remembers this, somebody upset him. It happened in the ward, and old John come at me with a pitchfork!

John: Yes, I did!

Dorothy: Did you? Actually I think I remember that story from before. [Hubbub: background laughter and chat.]

John: He started it!

Brian: . . . . and I was going round a corner, on four wheels, and broke a tooth . . . .

Dorothy: What's that?

Brian: . . . . and it stopped, and I went over its head ....

Dorothy: I haven't got that story, you'll have to tell us again, I'm afraid.

Brian: I fell off it, that's what happened.

(Tape transcript, meeting 16)

George was telling the John-and-pitchfork story, Brian the falling-off-a-bear story, and they clashed. George had the benefit, on that occasion, of a directly involved listener, John, and some noisy supporters from the sidelines. Brian was on his own. Nevertheless both stories were eventually disentangled and told, and both appear in the *Past Times* book. The extract demonstrated that story-telling was about *process* – getting the floor and holding it – as much as it was about content, and what the story actually conveyed.

Story-telling can be seen as an essential human activity. It is international, transhistorical and transcultural. It is simply there, like life itself (Barthes, 1977). It was there in the Past Times project in a way which linked this group of people with learning disabilities with people everywhere.

The nature and content of stories

The stories told in the group had many classical 'narrative features' (Finnegan, 1992, p. 172). They were clearly bounded, and framed, narratives. They contained characters, including the narrator himself; they portrayed an event, or episode, or a series of events and episodes; they featured a sequence of moves or actions; and they were often spoken in different voices, with other voices heard in dialogue with the narrator. Sometimes the story also conveyed some sort of moral or message. These were narrative features that I noted overall in the stories which were told – they were not necessarily all present in every story. The performance element of story-telling, and the audience-effect, meant that the stories became more complex over time with increased exposure and practice.

Stories represented themes which were important in the group. The story-tellers, in that sense, were performing another social function: conveying those messages and meanings which were important to other group members and – sometimes – to the group as a whole. There were *many* stories told, too many to recount here. They did, however, fall into four main themes, each of which can be explored with reference to examples. The themes were: 'boys will be boys'; dramatic moments (in a humdrum life); debunking authority figures; and turning the tables. I will look at each in turn, and I will do so using examples taken from the *Past Times* book rather than from transcripts. The stories in the book are in their final, and finished, form – the form in which they were intended for the outside world.

1 'Boys will be boys!'

Although other people in the group spoke about mischief and misfortune in their childhood, somehow George and Brian laid special claim to this territory. Mischief often took the form of getting back at a school teacher, as they were both happy to regale to others in the group.

Extract 55

George: The teacher comes round to me and clips my earhole. I says, 'Enough of that mister'. He says, 'What are you going to do about it?' I said, 'If you keep hitting me, you'll see'. He hit me because I told him to take his dannel. That's real village talk that is!

Brian: There was a board duster when I was at school. And there was a teacher once who threw the board duster at me! And I threw it back! I had my desk lid open, I was behind my desk lid. 'I was getting a book out of my desk, Miss.' Then she threw the board duster at me. I threw it back but it missed her. I threw it from my desk. It went on her desk, it did, it missed her. She gave me another chance, she didn't tell the headmaster . . . .

(Past Times, pp. 16-17)

In their stories, at least, George and Brian were able to challenge authority, and fight back where they could, even as schoolboys. Several classical narrative features are present: characters, scenes, moves and dialogue. And the moral of these stories? I have put them here as classical boys' stories, but they are on a universal and adult theme, of challenging authority – it's a theme which George returns to in stories from his adult life when he also fought back.

'Boys' stories' were also tales of misfortunes from childhood, when things went dramatically wrong. These were told with relish and humour and, it seemed, for the entertainment of others.

Extract 56

George: We had tricycles years ago. I tried one but I got to the bottom of the hill and I misjudged it, and I went over the top of the handlebars! I fell amongst some sheep. Some old farmer was getting some sheep out of the field and, of course, I didn't know they were there. He didn't half holler at me! 'Boy!' he said, 'Where do you think you're going?' He come and picked me up. He said, 'Are you all right?' I said, 'Yes'. He said, 'You should be more careful, you'll be hurting yourself'.

Then I thought, 'Well, it's not going to master me', so I got up and had another go. And I was steadier that time, I got to the bottom of the hill. I took it home and I said to my dad, 'How do you think I got on with this? I nearly broke my neck!'

(Past Times, p. 81)

Again there is action, drama and dialogue in this story. And a moral too, where George decided he was not going to be 'mastered' by his tricycle – he tries again and, in so doing, ultimately triumphs. Not to be outdone, Brian told a similar story of adversity, where he also found himself thrown through the air.

Extract 57

Brian: I had a bear on wheels. I was coming round a corner on the bear and I went down a slope, round the corner to the shop. I didn't know it was there, and instead of taking it slow, I must have pulled a string on its back and it growled and I went flying over its head. That's how I broke my front tooth. I went right down to the shop on it, and I pulled its string and 'grrrrr . . . .!' it growled. And I lost my tooth 'cos I went over his head, flying.

(Past Times, p. 82)

This is a similar dramatic incident, with action, drama and sound effects. It is not a story of triumph over adversity, however, it's a simple tale of misfortune – and a lost front tooth to show for it. Brian did not emerge a hero in his story but he told it well enough to cause much merriment in his audience.

2 Dramatic moments

There were many dramatic moments recalled and recounted in the Past Times group. Brian enjoyed telling stories – often against himself – of misfortunes similar to the bear incident. One such was the 'flattened flowers' story:

Extract 58

Brian: I remember how I used to help the milkman. I was going round with him one morning and it was quite black 'cos it was early morning. I was trying to get over this fence with the milk bottles in my hand and I missed my step and fell over. I landed in the flowers, I did! I squashed the flowers! I flattened 'em, I did! They didn't know who it were, 'cos we'd finished by then, and they didn't know. It were quite dark then.

            What we were doing was – it was quite dark – and we'd go over one fence and then another. It was too far to walk, so

we'd climb over, and down the other side. And then I fell in t'
flowers! And tumbled 'em all down.

(Past Times, p. 47)

There were many other dramatic moments in Brian's life, recaptured in the
group and printed in *Past Times*. George kept his end up with his tales of his
boyhood and adolescent years, such as the occasion when he spilled the
farmer's milk and, another time, when he let the air out of the policeman's
bicycle tyres. But the dramatic moments in his life took on a different aspect
when he recalled them from his hospital days. Ostensibly they were of a more
serious kind, with the threat or possibility of violence. Even so they were told
as funny stories – and everybody laughed.

Sometimes the threat was from another (male) patient. These stories – often
including members of George's audience – were very popular in the group.
To illustrate the point, I include two very similar stories, one involving
Albert, the other involving John. The props – pitchfork and shovel – are also
closely related. Were these stories based on real incidents, or were they
apocryphal?

Extract 59

George: I don't know who had upset Albert one particular morning but
we were going to work on the garden, and Albert got a
bloomin' pitchfork. He run after me and he was going to hit
me on top of my head with a pitchfork! Somebody had upset
him, I don't know who. I said, 'Albert, what's wrong with
you?' I hadn't even talked to him! I was just going to and, as I
say, he come at me with a pitchfork. The gardener come
through and said, 'Hey! What are you doing with that fork?'

(Past Times, p. 47)

Extract 60

George: Someone upset John one Monday afternoon and he went
running after me with a bloomin' shovel! He came round with
a shovel! I wondered who it was behind me. Someone said to
me, 'Look out, he's got a bloomin' shovel!'

I said to John, 'What's up John?' 'Oh sorry George', he said,
'you're the wrong one!' He said, 'I wanted old George
Armstrong. I thought you were old George Armstrong'. John
used to hate the sight of old George Armstrong, didn't you

John? He did hit poor old George, he didn't mean to hit him so hard, the poor old bugger – excuse my language – the poor old devil got hit by a wooden spade. He nearly killed the poor old bugger!

I don't know what he said to him. I said to him, 'What's up John?' 'Old Armstrong', he said, 'the old bugger, he's always upsetting me!' I said, 'I bet he won't next time!' He said, 'I'll kill him next time!'

(Past Times, pp. 74-75)

These were well-crafted stories. They had all the features of a narrative – characters, action, drama, dialogue and, in the second story, a punch-line; and they were well told, to an appreciative audience. Was life really so violent in the long-stay hospitals? Or were these simply moments when tempers flared, and frustration surfaced, in an otherwise unchanging and humdrum world? My impression was that, mostly, life *wasn't* like that – it was routine and repetitive. Those incidents stood out in people's memories as moments in time when life suddenly and unexpectedly took a sideways lurch. Order was soon restored but the incidents were remembered. Perhaps they had been recalled and re-told over the years and had passed into hospital folklore.

3 Debunking authority figures

Of course, in their stories of schooldays, members of the group recalled incidents with catapults, ink and rotten apples, where teachers were at the receiving end of well-aimed missiles. The debunking of authority figures in adult life often took the form, in the group, of retrospective denunciation. They were named, criticized and denounced. In earlier sections of the book, I highlighted an exchange between Margaret and George about the two ward sisters who, for years, had tyrannized and dominated the patients in their care. George and Margaret, with the agreement of others, had denounced Smith and Moffat as 'devils'. George went on, with encouragement, to denounce others who had similarly oppressed them.

Extract 61

Bill: There was an old bloke, when we were at Hasells Hall, who wouldn't give any money away. He was tight.

George: His name was Gilmore. Him and another bloke, old Bill didn't use to like him. His name was Carpenter, he come from Leicester, and old Bill and him, they was always quarrelling.

120

Bill:	He was a nasty old bloke. Smoke, smoke, smoke! It killed him in the end!
George:	I don't know if Bert still remembers Lewis? He was a Charge Nurse. He used to have three stripes on each arm and three pips on the top of his jacket. And first thing in the morning you knew he was about. If you said anything, and he went like that [raises his arm], you knew what he meant. Bed! He was a bugger first thing in the morning. You ask Bert. When we got to know him – you know – well, you'd know that he was the boss and nobody else. Once you got to know him he wasn't too bad. He'd let you know that he was in charge.
John:	Oh ar!
George:	A bloke called Hardy was next to him. 'Course Hardy left there before his time for robbing the patients. He was found out. The Super walked into the stores and Hardy was taking the tobacco and fags out of the coats. 'Course the doctor in charge said, 'Good evening, Mr Hardy. How much baccy and fags have you got in your pockets?' Hardy said, 'I've not got any, sir'. Old Bennett said, 'Turn your pockets out, Hardy, let's have a look!' Oh, he'd got I don't know how many baccy and fags. 'I think you'd better come to my office with me', old Bennett said, 'and tell me about it'. Hardy got sacked. He got the sack there and then.

(Past Times, pp. 64-65)

These were authority figures in the lives of group members. George even describes the quasi-military insignia sported by Lewis. They were, in reality, less than honourable people, who misused their power, and abused the powerless. It was only now, many years later, when the staff who had transgressed could be brought to book by a process of public denunciation. Samuel and Thompson (1990) suggest that people's inner hopes and fears can find expression through the idealization and demonization of the characters in their lives. In her accounts, Margaret had idealized those staff members who had shown warmth and kindness towards her. In joint accounts, she and others – led by George – demonized notorious ward sisters who had shown 'wickedness' towards them. They were denounced as 'devils' and deserved to die. So did Carpenter. Hardy got the sack for stealing from patients and equally deserved his fate.

Denunciation, and debunking, of staff came years after the event and came only through the telling of the story. It was a retrospective balancing of the books, necessary, but not ideal. Better still were those remembered occasions when the tables had been turned at the time and the staff member had been left looking foolish. These were very satisfying stories to tell, and to hear. They featured a kind of role reversal where the doctor, charge nurse, superintendent, and even the superintendent's wife, emerged from the incident as 'the fool'. The perpetrator – usually George but sometimes Bert or Albert – was the hero.

George's bike-in-the-chimney story, which I included earlier in another context, was one example of the role reversal. But there were several others, including the following two examples of the genre – both told by George.

Extract 62

George: We used to have cats down the farm and Dr Bennett, the Superintendent, he used to have his wife come and feed 'em twice a day. She'd come in the morning and at night, about quarter to five. And there used to be a bloke known as Bob Ward, he was under old Baxter (farm bailiff), but he wasn't a bad bloke, old Bob wasn't. He used to say he was just an ordinary workman. Anyway I remember she come down one Friday to feed the cats and I said, 'Bob,' I said, 'Old madam's coming down . . . .!' 'Where is she?' he said.   'Look   out', he said, 'I'll get the hose pipe'. Of course, old Bob when he got the hose pipe, he said, 'Turn her on boy!' I said 'OK, Bob', and I turned it on. I said, 'You'll kill that poor woman, Bob!' 'That doesn't matter', he said.

Bob didn't know that old Bennett, her husband, was behind her and, of course, the water knocked his hat off and she lost her handbag. Bob was a good old boy. He didn't think the doctor, the Super, was with her this certain afternoon. He swilled her, and got old Bennett wet an' all. He nearly went wild, he didn't half go on!

(*Past Times*, p. 67)

In this story, George collaborates with one of the hired farm hands to bring down – literally – the superintendent's wife. The incident had other unintended consequences but it was told in the spirit of turning the tables on authority. George told that story for – and against – himself. But he was also prepared to tell other stories where the action belonged to someone else.

Extract 63

George: Albert didn't tell you about the bucket of water he put over Baxter's office door, did he? Come on Albert, tell 'em! No one will hurt you, come on tell 'em . . . .

Well, there's a little nail at the top of the door, and there was big handles on the bucket, and I don't know how Albert got it on there without bending the handles . . . . Baxter saw him in there, and said, 'What are you doing in there Albert?' 'I'm going to water the flowers!' He had a great big bucket of water! 'I'm going to water the flowers, and then I'm going to water him!' Poor old Baxter came in – I hid behind the corner – old Baxter pushed his door shut and, 'course, he got water all over him!

Bob Ward comes in and says, 'What's up with old Jim?' I said, 'Look at him. He's been drownded!' He said, 'Ask Albert, he might know something about it!'

(Past Times, p. 69)

Are these adult versions of the boys-will-be-boys, boys' own stories? Are they reminiscent of all anti-authority stories of school and institutions everywhere and at all times? At one level they are; they could be the japes and high jinks from many boys' stories, even though group members would not have any first hand knowledge of them. There is something universal, and timeless, about the bringing down of 'the enemy', not violently but through the cleansing process of cold water.

Myths or truths?

Myths are universal, according to Samuel and Thompson (1990); they are the stuff of national beliefs and stories (Robin Hood, Dick Whittington and many other 'heroes'). They can convey magical feelings, conjure up fantasy fears and demonize enemies. They are so integral to human experience that they become part of everyday personal and collective memories. Life stories become imbued with myths to such an extent that they can become a 'personal mythology' in themselves, a means of 'self justification' (Samuel and Thompson, 1990, p. 10).

The telling of life stories through the oral tradition brings us close to the use, even the development, of myths. This is because oral narratives are ideally suited to convey moral values in the process of recounting actual events (Samuel and Thompson, 1990, p. 10). These stories can become 'parables', which come to exemplify courage, kindness or strength. They can also become fantasies, such as the 'revenge fantasy' of oppressed people, when they, in truth or fiction, turn the tables on their oppressors.

What about the stories regaled in the Past Times group? Were they myths – or truths? Or both? Myths, by their very nature and their universality, are hard to detect. However, it is likely that myths did play a part in the shaping and telling of stories in the group, even where these stories themselves were based on actual events. This does not invalidate the stories. Far from it. They become part of a common and universal human capacity to make sense of a sometimes sense-less past. Any myths which were created, or subscribed to, in the group were almost certainly embedded in real experience.

The best place to start, perhaps, is with that real experience. Even at this point, though, there is a sense in which group members were influenced by myths. This is because they were, during much of this century, part of the prevailing mythology – the 'folk devils' of their time who, by their very existence, fuelled the moral panic of the degenerating national stock. What sort of personal, and collective effect does this sort of categorization have on the people who were those mythical figures in the imagination of others? It is impossible to gauge the emotional effect of this process, but perhaps it influenced, somehow, the way people thought about and interpreted their experiences – and the way in which these experiences were later recounted as stories.

The stories, as we have seen, did more than convey actual events – they told other stories too. They were, in essence, stories of survival, where oppressed people survived their powerless position and endured the everyday humiliation at the hands of their oppressors. Not only did they survive, they laughed about it – developing a dark sense of humour about themselves and their oppressors, and the humiliation they were able to inflict on the 'enemy'. At least in retrospect, and in the telling, the stories conveyed a rich vein of defiance; these were strong, brave people who defied the worst aspects of a tyrannical regime. In their survival stories, and in their use of humour and defiance, group members were emulating the coping strategies of persecuted minority groups everywhere. According to Samuel and Thompson (1990, p. 19), people who are persecuted build up common threads, or myths, based on the survival of defeat or humiliation; and they use humour too to cope with disaster, and tell stories based on acts of defiance. Minority groups need these collective memories, or myths, to give people a sense of identity, and reinforce a sense of self; and to help in the everyday business of survival.

Chanfrault-Duchet suggests that people subscribe both to individual and collective myths (1991). The articulation between them means that the speaker, the narrator, can present her or himself as a social actor – as an individual person who is part of, and involved in, history. The Past Times project, which aimed to combine individual life stories with shared experiences, was bound to lead us into the realm of myths. Group members were, after all, engaged in giving meaning to their lives, and making sense of their experience, both separately and together. Not surprisingly, the emphasis was on survival and, ultimately, triumph. They did not look back on a 'Golden Age' when life was wonderful, and reflect on the loss of that 'Eden' or 'Paradise'. Of course, I had tried to invent one for them, a personal 'Golden Age' prior to hospitalization. But that did not work; myths have to have their basis in truth. The group members' journey was not from light into darkness, but a journey from darkness into light. The past served as a 'negative benchmark' in their case, and a means by which their later acts could be seen in terms of achievement rather than loss (Samuel and Thompson, 1990, p. 9).

Perhaps it's not a question of truth *or* myth, as I posed it at the beginning of this section, but a matter of truth *and* myth. Life is about both. *Past Times* was about both. The myth is, after all, the universalization of the 'truth' in a narrative format. And myths have their place in human experience. They derive from it, and they help shape it.

10 Reflections on practice

In this concluding chapter I want to look at research practice. This includes my own practice, and will involve a process of reflective reconsideration of the Past Times project – a critical look at what I set out to do, and what actually happened. I set out with high hopes, and high principles, but without any real idea of where I was going, or how I would know when (if) I got there. Was my own journey 'out of darkness into light' really necessary? Or could I have planned it better? Can this research project shed light on other people's research plans? Are there implications here for research practice more generally?

My final task is to look ahead. After all, the classic ending to a research report is to ask 'what next?', and to look at what research still needs to be done in the chosen field. This book is no exception. I end with the future, therefore, looking ahead to what possible developments there might be in auto/biographical research.

Looking back

When I set up what was then called my history group, I had three aims in mind. My starting point was to test a method, to see if and how an auto/biographical research approach could be used with people with learning disabilities. Assuming that techniques drawn from oral history would actually work in this context then, of course, I aimed to capture on tape, and in print, the stories which emerged. But I had another aim which went way beyond the telling of people's stories. It proved an elusive, though, in the end, an attainable aim, but it caused mystification throughout. My third aim was to make a start, at least, on co-constructing a joint historical account of their lives with members of the group.

I will look back at each of these aims in turn, and see how far they were achieved.

1 Testing a method

The method worked. It worked from the moment I sat down with the history group, switched my tape recorder on and invited people to talk about the past. They did so, sometimes at length, but often not in any way I had anticipated or planned.

There is no doubt in my mind that the auto/biographical approach works with people with learning disabilities. This at least has come out of this research, and I think it is a very important finding. There is more to it, however, than turning on the tape recorder and taking people through a set of universal, and 'safe' topics of ordinary life. This is what I attempted to do and the consequences, in terms of conflicting agendas and widespread mystification (including my own), have been highlighted throughout this book.

I chose a group setting because I wanted to engage people in working together in order to share memories and spark off ideas. I assumed, wrongly as it turned out, that a history group would be task-centred. None of those unsettling under-currents for us, as this was a research-focused group. We would, I was sure, sail serenely through, with my research aims to the fore, and my safe topics to keep us steady. The reality was, as I know now, quite different, as even research groups go through the same stages as all other groups, and we had our share of 'storming' and 'norming' before we got properly on to 'performing'. It had its conflicts and its leadership struggles, and it built up its own traditions in opposition to my aims.

The safe topics policy, as I have indicated throughout the book, was flawed. There were no safe areas, no hiding places. There were silences, as I discovered, and sometimes there was a need for creative listening, or 'listening beyond words' (Bertaux-Wiame, 1981, p. 260). In a sense I was a creative listener, listening for a joint account when it was not there, and not hearing the words of individual people speaking about their real lives rather than their 'ordinary lives'.

Looking back, and with the benefit of hindsight, what would I do differently now? As statements of intent my aims were fine; it was more in their application that they could be faulted. What I would do differently now would be to negotiate joint aims with research participants, rather than attempt to impose my own. I would also hope to be more open-minded about the research agenda, and what we talked about, rather than, again, imposing safe topics and ordinary lives on people.

On the whole, I think I would stick with the group format because it does allow other layers of understanding and insight to emerge between people, although I might introduce more one-to-one and mini-group work to allow individuals to talk in more depth. I would go to group sessions better prepared, however, with a co-leader if possible but, failing that, with a supportive person to debrief with afterwards. I would certainly keep my reflective diary as a way of attempting to make sense of what, at the time, often seemed to be a fragmented, and arbitrary, set of exchanges between people.

The other thing that I would do differently now is to think about time more realistically. I had originally assumed that I could do some quick research, simply testing a method over a few weeks. This was unrealistic but so too, for many people, would be the two years that I eventually spent. It took so long because of my unpreparedness. We needed time, as all groups do, to develop trust and commitment, but we also needed time to sort out our conflicting agendas. This took a long time but we got there. The sense of togetherness which then prevailed, however, meant that the group developed a life and momentum of its own. And this took more time . . . .

2   Facilitating stories

The Past Times project generated stories. It generated multiple stories, at different levels, for different purposes and told in many voices. It generated, at my behest, stories of ordinary lives and period details of the past. It generated, at the behest of group members, stories of loss, separation and segregation. In that sense, the project succeeded. It enabled those lost voices of people with learning disabilities to be heard, and acknowledged, and made it possible for hitherto invisible people to be seen and known. It enabled people to represent themselves, to be seen as fully rounded human beings with a personal past and not just as victims of an oppressive system. The project brought out those things which people with learning disabilities share, and have in common, with other people, as well as charting where their lives had taken a different course.

It did all this and more. The project was fun. The group was, on the whole, a good place to be. It brought warmth, support, understanding and insight to everyone, including myself. The decision to end it was one of the most difficult I have ever taken in a research context. The group provided time and space for people to talk. It was an opportunity to remember past events, to share them and to reflect on them. It was a facilitative group.

My role was meant to be facilitative but often it was not. In the early stages of the group, for all sorts of good reasons, I had wanted to focus on ordinary lives. Group members wanted to focus on real lives, as they had lived them.

One of the most striking insights of this project, for me, was the strength of people's wish, or need, to review their lives. This was their starting point. In any subsequent project I would understand and respect this wish, and make it my starting point too.

The other (re)discovery in this project was the importance of the written word. It was fine to sit around chatting, with a tape recorder taping our spoken words. But there was nothing to show for all this talk until I produced the first draft of the booklet *Past Times*. This transformed the group into 'our group' working on 'our book' to make it 'bigger and better'. In giving something back, in the form of a written document, I inadvertently facilitated a whole new set of stories, some of them told jointly just as I had hoped for when we had first set out. The written word, even if it could not be read personally, was seen as authoritative. It was more fixed and enduring than the spoken word, and it could be shown to others as a record of people's lives, a testimony to their survival.

The subsequent rounds of readings which followed this first draft led to the second and final versions of *Past Times*. The readings made all sorts of things possible. At one level, they were simply social occasions, as everyone enjoyed hearing their words read out and heard by an audience. At another level they had a practical function, allowing us to check details, and amend people's accounts as appropriate. But, most important of all, the readings inspired more memories, some of them shared, as people re-lived their account and had the chance – rare in research – to re-visit it. The group meetings had, themselves, encouraged people to be reflective; now the readings enhanced this process. Having the story there, already in words, meant it could be added to in the light of further memories, and/or it could be re-evaluated in terms of a new insight into its meaning.

On the face of it, the written word would seem less than central to people with learning disabilities. And yet that simply was not true. Although I had always intended to give feedback to group members, it took me a long time to do so. There were various reasons for the delay: there wasn't time, I was busy transcribing tapes, I was unsure about how do it. In any subsequent project I would make time, by building it in – and give participants written feedback regularly so that they had a stake in how it evolved and how it was presented.

3 Co-constructing history

The Past Times project has contributed, albeit in a small way, to building a collective account of the lives of people with learning disabilities. This is important in terms of co-constructing a history of learning disability from below, through the eyes and experiences of those people who had lived that history. In this project people were oral historians, witnesses of an era which was now passing. Without their accounts, and the accounts of others, there would be no record of that lived history – only the documentary history written by others about key events, dates and 'great men'.

A collective account did emerge in the group, ranging from everyday personal and social period details, to auto/biographical and shared accounts of life in long-stay hospitals. Group members proved to be good oral historians, drawing on details of national and local policy and practice which were verifiable from secondary sources.

The group format was, of course, a key factor in the development of a collective account; so too was the written document *Past Times* in its various drafts. The group gave people a forum in which to speak, an audience to address, and co-witnesses to verify what they said or, sometimes, to challenge it. The book, in its several manifestations, was a reminder of how far we had come, and a spur to do more. The spur for group members was to 'tell it how it was', to let people know what life had been like for them. This was the beginning of an historical awareness that individual pasts were part of a much bigger historical picture, and that their lives had been shaped by social forces beyond their control.

Part of the life review process was, of course, to make sense of individual lives and experiences. Part of the sharing of memories process which occurred in the group was to make sense of all their lives. This took the form of capturing factual details, and recording them, but also took the form of re-visiting scenes and people from the past. This was the story-telling tradition which emerged in the group, and which made it possible to reconsider past oppressions and to denounce those responsible.

Initially it was my wish that we should work together on co-constructing history. That wish later came to be shared, but it took a long time. There was a prior need, it seemed, for individual group members to make sense of their own lives first before seeing those lives in a wider context. The historical account is not, therefore, as strong as it might have been had we worked on it together from an earlier stage.

What the group discovered for itself was an interest, and a stake, in history, and a wish to know more. This drive to know, and to understand, a shared past as well as individual histories could be better harnessed in any subsequent project. It needs to made explicit at the outset, and owned as an aim by everyone. At the same time, it would probably pay to allocate space and time for the life review process which could otherwise sabotage the historical quest. And historical awareness probably benefits from nurturing; for example, finding out more together through site visits, interviews with key informants and looking at newspaper cuttings and other documents from the past.

Implications for practice

The project raised, for me, two areas of research practice which are of overriding importance in auto/biographical research: ownership and reflexivity. I will look briefly at each of these aspects of practice.

The question of ownership runs through all qualitative research projects. Mostly researchers, and/or funding bodies, own research. In feminist, participative and disability research, however, ownership is a contested area. If life stories are recounted, taped and transcribed as part of someone else's research, then whose lives are they? Technically the tapes are the property of the interviewee, but the auto/biography may be edited, cut, themed, and put alongside others, to prove or illustrate a point in a report or book which is written by the researcher. There is increasingly now a counter-bid for ownership, not just of the tape of one's life, but for a stake in the research of which it forms part.

The question of ownership is less clear-cut in learning disability research, however, where people with learning disabilities are less likely to claim a stake in the research or its outcome. The research may be about them, it may concern their lives, past and present, and it may have consequences for them – but how does it become theirs? The Past Times project was my initiative. I had the idea, and invited people to join a history group based on my agenda and aims. In all those ways I owned the research. And yet the group, and its members, separately and together had ideas and aims of their own, and we struggled towards a joint ownership, and a shared product, the book *Past Times*. Perhaps our struggles would have been less had we established joint ownership at the outset. It's nice to think so.

Some researchers have begun to explore the possibilities of working together with people with learning disabilities on research projects which are about their lives and concerns. Examples such as work on consulting with children, working with people with learning disabilities to look at gender issues in day care, and exploring accessible ways of disseminating research findings, have been reported (Minkes, *et al.*, 1995; Townsley, 1995). Other researchers have considered how ownership of research might be transferred through, for example, a process of 'reverse commodification', where the researcher puts their skills at the disposal of participants to work with them rather than study them in an 'objective' way (Ramcharan and Grant, 1994). One of the things I felt most strongly in the Past Times project was that ownership passed from me to the group when I produced the first draft of the book. At that point I became the group's scribe, perhaps even its servant; my skills were at the group's disposal.

My next point regarding good research practice concerns reflexivity. Auto/biographical research requires a reflective approach. Getting immersed

131

in the lives of other people can bring with it, as I know only too well, the feeling of being submerged. The additional complications in the Past Times project was the group itself, and those mysterious under-currents which swept us first one way, and then another. There was no escaping this immersion, or threatened submersion; auto/biographical research means using one's self as the main research tool. This requires self and other awareness, and an openness to what is happening, even while it happens (Atkinson and Shakespeare, 1993). This is research reflexivity in action: 'Being sensitive to both our informants and our own feelings, perceptions and speech will make us more able to hear their stories' (Goodley, 1996, p. 339). That is true enough, but it is difficult to put into practice at the time.

What is just as important, perhaps more so, is the capacity to be reflective, and critically aware afterwards, when looking back at research encounters. For this reason it is a good idea to keep a reflective diary, in order to monitor one's role and input to the process. The reflective diary is seen as a crucial research tool in itself in related areas of study. Judith Okely, for example, sees the anthropologist's diary as the place to explore new insights and develop self-awareness (1992). Self-definition, and self-exploration, are an integral part of the research process, according to Malcolm Crick, to such an extent that one's self must have 'a focal place in our writings' (1992, p. 175).

The following extract from my research diary pinpoints that moment in the group when I felt we had chatted long enough and it was now time to *do* something. I was probably right, as this report was written at the end of the fifteenth session! It was summer time, time to take a break – but also time to do a review.

Extract 64

This was a review session but it wasn't easy. I asked in several different ways what they'd thought about the project/group; what it had meant to them; what they had liked/not liked. I got a series of comments like 'It was all right' (John) and 'It killed time' (George). Every time I asked that sort of question, Brian didn't answer directly, he went off into an instant reminiscence. I felt sure this was his way of saying, 'Yes, I liked it, I'd like to go on and do some more'. The direct question and answer approach just didn't work.

Then I wondered what *product* they'd like – a book perhaps? I showed them the Anthology, '*Know Me As I Am*', and *Secret Lives*. I read out some of Brenda Cook's work on memories, and they really liked it: 'We had one of those!' (Clothes pulley in the kitchen.) I read out a hospital memory from *Secret Lives* and they listened intently. They weren't sure what to think. I passed the books around.

One of the problems for them, I realized, was how to associate what we'd done (chat) with what's done in books. We haven't *done* anything, there's nothing to show for our labours – except in my notes. This was my cue. We need to take a break anyway because of holidays, but during that break I need to do some homework. My job is to transform sound into words on paper so there's something to look at.

(Diary extract)

The next time we met, of course, I was able to present everyone with their first draft copy of *Past Times*: their words, and their work.

Looking forward

This book is, in essence, the story of one research project. It contains, as we have seen, many stories and several voices within the one main story. This attention to the 'lost voices' of people with learning disabilities would have been unthinkable at other junctures in the history of this century. It becomes possible now as part of wider changes, not only in the learning disability field, but beyond it in society as a whole. Auto/biographical research reflects those wider changes and begins to add new voices to help shape their direction. In looking forward to the future of auto/biographical research, it is necessary first to look at its present credentials; at where it is now, and why. Only then can we look at where it might be going, and what the future might hold.

Auto/biographical research is a late twentieth century phenomenon. It can be seen as one manifestation of wider changes sweeping society in its so-called 'post modernity' phase. Modernity itself was characterized by certainty, a certainty that the application of reason and rationality would lead to scientific change and economic progress, and that grand schemes could bring about lasting and beneficial change. In the learning disability field, the identification of 'mental deficiency', and its 'treatment' in institutions, was an expression of modernity and 'modern' thinking. Whilst the early asylums aspired to be 'symbols of progress and therapy', later concessions to the widespread demand for the control of mental defectives led to institutions becoming 'hidden places', literally at the margins of society (Radford, 1994, p. 11).

The professions of medicine and psychology became important in the quest, first, for care and, later, for containment and control. Over time institutions fell into disrepute. 'Experts' became less revered. Measurement, classifications and the treatment of 'deficits' looked more suspect. The post-modern phase in learning disability came with the growing realization that institutions, and experts, had failed people with learning disabilities. Normalization heralded the demise of modernity in the learning disability field. It challenged the old certainties about institutional care. Ironically, though, it instituted new certainties of its own to do with integration and conformity and helped establish a new set of experts. Normalization's assertions about the lives of people with learning disabilities have themselves been challenged in the 1990s.

In this post-modern era, certainty has given way to fragmentation and diversity. Now 'there are no overarching truths, no scientific answers' (Williams, 1996, p. 63). It is in this context that it has become possible to move from ideas about universalism, and standardization, for example, to a recognition that people are actually different and have diverse needs. With that recognition of diversity comes the 'possibility of people articulating their own needs' (Williams, 1992, p. 10). The growth of self-advocacy, and the greater involvement of people with learning disabilities in the design and delivery of community-based services, are manifestations of this articulation of individual needs.

At the same time, of course, people in the self-advocacy movement, and beyond, have begun to speak up about their experiences as people with learning disabilities as well as their needs as service users. Their auto/biographical accounts have helped counteract stereotypes about who and what they are, and they have begun to emerge as people with a diversity of backgrounds and experiences. The sweeping away of old certainties, and authoritative voices, has made a space for other voices to be heard. Auto/biographical research has helped create that space, and has helped ensure that those newer, and sometimes less certain, voices are heard.

This is not the end of the story. Even in a project which I initiated and ran, the participants were, in the end, able to use the situation to tell their individual and linked stories by using my research skills. They harnessed my skills of listening, recording, transcribing and editing to work on their 'bigger and better' version of *Past Times*. The group members thus showed research awareness, as well as historical awareness, and made the first step towards changing the classic power relationship between researcher and subjects which characterizes most research. They were there, by my invitation, to be participants in my project, but they subsequently became much more active shapers of that research agenda – an example, perhaps, of a modest shift towards 'emancipatory research' (Zarb, 1992).

Auto/biographical accounts can harness the reflexivity of people with learning disabilities, and heighten their historical awareness. As research awareness grows, so more people are likely to become involved in the telling of their personal histories, and thus in the telling of history itself. Those accounts, separately and together, will help tell the history of learning disability in this century. The challenge that still remains is how that history is presented, and to whom – and how it properly becomes a history that is known and owned by people with learning disabilities themselves.

Bibliography

Amans, D. and Darbyshire, C. (1989) 'A voice of our own' in Brechin, A. and Walmsley, J. (eds) *Making Connections: Reflecting on the lives and experiences of people with learning difficulties*. Hodder and Stoughton, London.

Atkinson, D. (1988) 'Research interviews with people with mental handicaps', *Mental Handicap Research*, 1, 1, 75-90.

Atkinson, D. (1989) 'Group Homes for People with Mental Handicap: Key Issues for Everyday Living' in Brown, A. and Clough, R. (eds) *Groups and Groupings. Life and Work in Day and Residential Centres*. Tavistock/Routledge, London.

Atkinson, D. (1993a) *Past Times*. Milton Keynes, private publication.

Atkinson, D. (1993b) 'Relating' in Shakespeare, P., Atkinson, D. and French, S. (eds) *Reflecting on Research Practice. Issues in Health and Social Welfare*. Open University Press, Buckingham.

Atkinson, D. (1993c) 'Life History Work with a Group of People with Learning Disabilities'. *Groupwork*, 6, 3, 199-210.

Atkinson, D. (1994) '"I got put away": Group-based reminiscence with people with learning difficulties', in Bornat, J. (ed.) *Reminiscence Reviewed: Evaluations, achievements, perspectives*. Open University Press Buckingham.

Atkinson, D. and Shakespeare, P. (1993) 'Introduction' in Shakespeare, P., Atkinson, D. and French, S. (eds) *Reflecting on Research Practice. Issues in Health and Social Welfare*. Buckingham, Open University Press.

Atkinson, D. and Walmsley, J. (1995) 'A woman's place? Issues of gender' in Philpot, T. and Ward, L. (eds) *Values and Visions. Changing Ideas in Services for People with Learning Difficulties*. Butterworth-Heinemann, Oxford.

Atkinson, D. and Walmsley, J. (1997) 'Using Auto/Biographical Approaches with People with Learning Difficulties': *Auto/Biography*, forthcoming.

Atkinson, D. and Williams, F. (eds) (1990) *'Know Me As I Am'. An anthology of prose, poetry and art by people with learning difficulties.* London, Hodder and Stoughton.

Barker, D. (1989) 'The Biology of Stupidity: Genetics, Eugenics and Mental Deficiency in the Inter-War Years'. *British Journal for the History of Science,* 22, 347-375.

Barthes, R. (1977) *Roland Barthes* (translated by Richard Howard). Macmillan Press, London.

Bedford Group Hospital Management Committee (1960) *Bedford Group of Hospitals, Survey 1948-1959,* Bedford Group HMC, Bedford.

Benmayor, R. (1991) 'Testimony, Action Research and Empowerment: Puerto Rican Women and Popular Education', in Gluck, S. B. and Patai, D. (eds) *Women's Words. The Feminist Practice of Oral History.* Routledge, London.

Bertaux, D. (1981) 'From the life history approach to the transformation of sociological practice', in Bertaux, D. (ed.) *Biography and Society: The life history approach in the social sciences.* Sage, Beverly Hills and London.

Bertaux-Wiame, I. (1981) 'The life history approach to the study of internal migration', in Bertaux, D. (ed.) *Biography and Society: The life history approach in the social sciences.* Sage, Beverly Hills and London.

Birren, J E. and Deutchman, D.E. (1991) *Guided Autobiography Groups for Older Adults. Exploring the Fabric of Life.* John Hopkins University Press, Baltimore and London.

Bogdan, R. and Taylor, S. (1976) 'The judged, not the judges: an insider's view of mental retardation'. *American Psychologist,* 31, 47-52.

Bogdan, R. and Taylor, S.J. (1982) *Inside Out: The Social Meaning of Retardation.* University of Toronto Press, Toronto.

Booth, T. and Booth, W. (1994) *Parenting under Pressure. Mothers and fathers with learning difficulties.* Open University Press, Buckingham.

Bornat, J. (1989) 'Oral History as a Social Movement: Reminiscence and Older People'. *Oral History,* 17, 2, 16-24.

Bornat, J. (1992) 'The Communities of Community Publishing'. *Oral History,* 20, 2, 23-31.

Bornat, J. and Walmsley, J. (1994) 'Oral history with vulnerable people: challenges to concepts and practice'. Conference paper, New York, International Conference on Oral History.

Burnside, M. (1991) *My Life Story.* Pecket Well College, Halifax.

Chanfrault-Duchet, M-F. (1991) 'Narrative Structures, Social Models, and Symbolic Representation in the Life Story', in Gluck, S.B. and Patai, D. (eds) *Women's Words. The Feminist Practice of Oral History.* Routledge, London.

137

Chappell, A.L. (1992) 'Towards a Sociological Critique of the Normalisation Principle'. *Disability, Handicap and Society*, 7, 1, 35-51.

Coleman, P. G. (1986) *Ageing and Reminiscence Processes: Social and Clinical Implications.* John Wiley, Chichester.

Cooper, M. (1997) 'Mabel Cooper's Life Story' in Atkinson, D., Jackson, M. and Walmsley, J. (eds) *Forgotten Lives. Exploring the History of Learning Disability.* BILD Publications, Kidderminster .

Cornwell, J. (1984) *Hard-earned Lives: Accounts of Health and Illness from East London.* Tavistock, London.

Crick, M. (1992) 'Ali and me. An essay in street-corner anthropology', in Okely, J. and Callaway, H. (eds) *Anthropology and Autobiography*, Routledge, London.

Davis, A., Eley, R., Flynn, M., Flynn, P. and Roberts, G. (1995). 'To have and have not: Addressing issues of poverty' in Philpot, T. and Ward, L. (eds) *Values and Visions. Changing Ideas in Services for People with Learning Difficulties.* Butterworth Heinemann, Oxford.

Deacon, J. (1974) *Tongue Tied.* NSMHC, London.

Department of Health and Social Security (1971) *Better Services for the Mentally Handicapped.* HMSO, London.

Diederich, N. (1994) 'The Career of People with Learning Difficulties: Behaviour patterns and identity'. Conference paper, Univ. of E. London.

Digby, A. (1996) 'Contexts and perspectives' in Wright, D. and Digby, A. (eds) *From Idiocy to Mental Deficiency. Historical perspectives on people with learning disabilities.* Routledge, London.

Downer, J. and Walmsley, J. (1997) 'Shouting the Loudest: Self Advocacy, Power and Diversity' in Ramcharan, P. (ed.) *Empowerment in Everyday Life.* Jessica Kingsley, London.

Edgerton, R B. (1967) *The Cloak of Competence.* University of California Press, Berkeley.

Edgerton, R.B. and Bercovici, S.M. (1976) 'The cloak of competence: years later', *American Journal of Mental Deficiency*, 80, 485-497.

Edgerton, R.B., Bollinger, M. and Herr, B. (1984) 'The cloak of competence: after two decades', *American Journal of Mental Deficiency*, 88, 345-351.

Etherington, A., Hall, K. and Whelan, E. (1988) 'What it's like for us ' in Towell, D. (ed.) *An Ordinary Life in Practice: Developing Comprehensive Community-Based Services for People with Learning Disabilities.* King's Fund Centre, London.

Fido, R. and Potts, M. (1989) '"It's not true what was written down!" Experiences of Life in a Mental Handicap Institution.' *Oral History*, 17, 2, 31-34.

138

Fielden, M.A. (1990) 'Reminiscence as a therapeutic intervention with sheltered housing residents: A comparative study'. *British Journal of Social Work*, 20, 1, 21-44.

Finch, J. (1984) 'It's great to have someone to talk to: The Ethics and Politics of Interviewing Women' in Bell, C. and Roberts, H. (eds) *Social Researching: Politics, Problems, Practice*. Routledge and Kegan Paul, London.

Finnegan, R. (1992) *Oral Traditions and the Verbal Arts. A guide to research practice*. Routledge, London.

Flynn, M. (1986) 'Adults who are mentally handicapped as consumers: issues and guidelines for interviewing' *Journal of Mental Deficiency Research*, 30, 369-377.

Flynn, M.C. (1989) *Independent Living for Adults with Mental Handicap: A Place of My Own*. Cassell, London.

Gibson, F. (1989) *Using Reminiscence: A Training Pack*. Help the Aged, London.

Goffman, E. (1963) *Stigma: on the management of spoiled identity*. Penguin, Harmondsworth.

Goffman, E. (1968) *Asylums. Essays on the Social Situation of Mental Patients and Other Inmates*. Penguin, Harmondsworth.

Goodley, D. (1996) 'Tales of Hidden Lives: A critical examination of life history research with people who have learning difficulties'. *Disability and Society*, 11, 3, 333-348.

Graham, H. (1984) 'Surveying through Stories' in Bell, C. and Roberts, H. (eds) *Social Researching: Politics, Problems, Practice*. Routledge and Kegan Paul, London.

Holman, B. (1987) 'Research from the underside' *British Journal of Social Work*, 17, 669-683.

Humphrey, R. (1993) 'Life Stories and Social Careers: Ageing and social life in an ex-mining town'. *Sociology*, 27, 1, 166-178.

Humphries, S. (1984) *The Handbook of Oral History: Recording Life Stories*. Inter-Action Trust, London.

Humphries, S. and Gordon, P. (1992) *Out of Sight: Recording the life stories of disabled people*. Channel 4 Publication, London.

Hunt, N. (1967) *The World of Nigel Hunt*. Darwen Finlayson, Beaconsfield.

Islington Disablement Association (1992) *Speak Out with Other People*. Islington Disablement Association, Islington.

Jackson, M. (1996) 'Institutional Provision for the Feeble-Minded in Edwardian England. Sandlebridge and the scientific morality of permanent care' in Wright, D. and Digby, A. (eds) *From Idiocy to Mental Deficiency. Historical perspectives on people with learning disabilities*. BILD Publications, Kidderminster.

Jackson, M. (1997) 'Images from the Past: Using photographs' in Atkinson, D., Jackson, M. and Walmsley, J. (eds). *Forgotten Lives: Exploring the history of learning disability.* Routledge. London.

Jahoda, A., Markova, I. and Cattermole, M. (1988) 'Stigma and the self-concept of people with a mild mental handicap', *Journal of Mental Deficiency Research,* 32, 103-115.

Jay Report, The (1979) *Report of the Committee of Enquiry into Mental Handicap Nursing and Care,* Vol. 1, Cmnd. 7469-1. HMSO, London.

Jones, G. (1986) *Social Hygiene in Twentieth Century Britain.* Croom Helm, London.

Khan, R.F. (1985) 'Mental retardation and paternalistic control' in Laura, R.S. and Ashman, A.F. (eds) *Moral Issues in Mental Retardation.* London, Croom Helm.

King's Fund Centre (1980) *An Ordinary Life.* King's Fund Centre, London.

Korman, N. and Glennerster, H. (1990) *Hospital Closures.* Open University Press, Milton Keynes.

Lawrence, J. and Mace, J. (1992) *Remembering in Groups. Ideas from Reminiscence and Literacy Work.* Oral History Society, London.

Luton Society for Parents of Backward Children (1968) *Year Book,* Luton Society for Parents of Backward Children, Luton.

Luton Society for Mentally Handicapped Children (1970) *Year Book,* Luton Society for Mentally Handicapped Children, Luton.

Mills, C.W. (1957) *The Sociological Imagination.* Oxford University Press, Oxford.

Minister, K. (1991) 'A Feminist Frame for the Oral History Interview', in Gluck, S B. and Patai, D. (eds) *Women's Words. The Feminist Practice of Oral History.* Routledge, London.

Minkes, J., Townsley, R., Weston, C. and Williams, C. (1995) 'Having a Voice: Involving People with Learning Difficulties in Research'. *British Journal of Learning Disabilities,* 23, 94-97.

Mitchell, P. (1997) 'Self Advocacy and Families', *Disability and Society* (forthcoming).

Morris, J. (1989) *Able Lives: Women's Experiences of Paralysis.* Women's Press, London.

Morris, J. (1991) *Pride Against Prejudice.* Women's Press, London.

Morris, P. (1969) *Put Away: A Sociological Study of Institutions for the Mentally Retarded.* Routledge and Kegan Paul, London.

National Council for Civil Liberties (1951) *50,000 Outside the Law.* NCCL, London.

Nirje, B. (1969) 'The normalisation principle and its human management implications' in Kugel, R. B. and Wolfensberger, W. (eds) *Changing Patterns in Residential Services for the Mentally Retarded*, Presidential Commission on Mental Retardation, Washington DC.

Oakley, A. (1981) 'Interviewing women: a contradiction in terms?' in Roberts, H. (ed) *Doing Feminist Research*. Routledge and Kegan Paul, London.

Okely, J. (1992) 'Anthropology and autobiography: participatory experience and embodied knowledge' in Okely, J. and Callaway, H. (eds) *Anthropology and autobiography*. Routledge, London.

Oliver, M. (1990) *The Politics of Disablement*. Macmillan Educational, Basingstoke.

Patai, D. (1991) 'US Academics and Third World Women: Is Ethical Research Possible?' in Gluck, S.B. and Patai, D. (eds) *Women's Words: The Feminist Practice of Oral History*. Routledge, London.

People First (1993) *Everything you ever wanted to know about safer sex*. People First, London.

People First (1993) *Oi, It's My Assessment*. People First, London.

Portelli, A. (1991) *The death of Luigi Trastulli: memory and other stories: form and meaning in oral history*. Suny Press, New York.

Potts, M. and Fido, R. (1991) *'A Fit Person To Be Removed'*. Northcote House, Plymouth.

Radford, J. (1991) 'Sterilization Versus Segregation: Control of the "Feebleminded", 1900-1938', *Social Sciences and Medicine*, 33, 4, 449-458.

Radford, J.P. (1994) 'Intellectual Disability and the Heritage of Modernity' in Rioux, M.H. and Bach, M. *Disability is not Measles. New Research Paradigms in Disability*. Roeher Institute, Ontario.

Ramcharan, P. and Grant, G. (1994) 'Setting One Agenda for Empowering Persons with a Disadvantage with the Research Process', in Rioux, M.H. and Bach, M. (eds) *Disability Is Not Measles. New Research Paradigms in Disability*. Roeher Institute, Ontario.

Ryan, J. (1980) *The Politics of Mental Handicap*. Penguin, Harmondsworth.

Samuel, R. and Thompson, P. (1990) 'Introduction' in Samuel, R. and Thompson, P. (eds) *The Myths We Live By*. Routledge, London.

Sigelman, C.K., Budd, E.C., Spanhel, C.L. and Scoenrock, C.J. (1981) 'When in doubt say yes: acquiescence in interviews with mentally retarded persons' *Mental Retardation*, 19, 53-58.

Spencer, D.A. (1990) *Meanwood Park Hospital, Leeds, Seventy Years, 1919-1989. A Chronicle*. Unpublished report.

Stacey, J. (1991) 'Can there be a feminist ethnography?' In Gluck, S.B. and Patai, D. (eds) *Women's Words: The Feminist Practice of Oral History.* Routledge, London.

Stainton, T. (1991) 'Legacy of our "caring" predecessors'. *Community Living,* October, 1991, 14-15.

Stainton, T. (1992) 'A terrible danger to the race'. *Community Living,* January, 1992, 18-20.

Stevens, A. (1995) 'Changing Attitudes to Disabled People in the Scout Association in Britain (1908-62): A contribution to a history of disability'. *Disability and Society,* 10, 3, 281-293.

Stevens, A. (1997) 'Recording the History of an Institution: The Royal Eastern Counties Institution at Colchester' in Atkinson, D., Jackson, M. and Walmsley, J. (eds) *Forgotten Lives: Exploring the History of Learning Disability.* BILD Publications, Kidderminster.

Thompson, P. (1988) *The Voice of the Past: Oral History* (2nd edition). Oxford University Press, Oxford.

Thomson, M. (1992) *The Problem of Mental Deficiency in England and Wales 1913-1946.* Unpublished D.Phil thesis, Oxford University.

Townsley, R. (1995) 'Avon Calling', *Community Care,* 12-18 January, 1995, 26-27.

Walmsley, J. (1990) 'The role of groupwork in research with people with learning difficulties'. *Groupwork,* 3, 1, 49-64.

Walmsley, J. (1993) 'Women First'. *Critical Social Policy,* Issue 38, 86-99.

Walmsley, J. (1994) *Gender, Caring and Learning Disability.* Unpublished PhD thesis, Open University.

Walmsley, J. (1996) 'Dwelling on Difference: Historical and personal representations of people with learning difficulties'. 1996 Oral History Society Conference paper.

Whittaker, A., Gardner, S. and Kershaw, J. (1990) *Service Evaluation by People with Learning Difficulties.* King's Fund Centre, London.

Wilkinson, J. (1990) '"Being there": evaluating life quality from feelings and daily experience' in Brechin, A. and Walmsley, J. (eds) *Making Connections: Reflecting on the lives and experiences of people with learning difficulties.* Hodder and Stoughton, London.

Williams, F. (1992) 'Somewhere over the rainbow: universality and diversity in social policy', in Manning, N. and Page, R. (eds) *Social Policy Review, 1991-92.* Social Policy Association, Canterbury.

Williams, F. (1993) *Social Policy, Social Divisions and Social Change.* Unpublished PhD Thesis, Open University.

Williams, F. (1996) 'Postmodernism, feminism and the question of difference', in Parton, N. (ed.) *Social Theory, Social Change and Social Work.* Routledge, London.

Williams, P. (1985) 'The Nature and Foundations of the Concept of Normalization' in Karas, E. (ed.) *Current Issues in Clinical Psychology, 2.* Plenum Press, New York.

Wolfensberger, W. (1972) *The Principle of Normalization in Human Services.* National Institute on Mental Retardation, Toronto.

Wolfensberger, W. (1975) *The Origin and Nature of Our Institutional Models.* Human Policy Press, Syracuse, New York.

Wolfensberger, W. (1980) 'The definition of normalization: update, problems, disagreements, and misunderstandings' in Flynn, R.J. and Nitsch, K.E. (eds) *Normalization, Social Integration, and Community Services.* University Park Press, Baltimore.

Wolfensberger, W. (1983) 'Social Role Valorization: a proposed new term for the principle of normalization', *Mental Retardation,* 21, 6, 234-239.

Wood Report, The (1929) *Report of the Mental Deficiency Committee* (Chairman: A. Wood). HMSO, London.

Wyngaarden, M. (1981) 'Interviewing Mentally Retarded Persons: Issues and Strategies' in Bruininks, R., Meyers, C., Sigford, B. and Lakin, K. C. (eds) *Deinstitutionalization and Community Adjustment of Mentally Retarded People.* American Association on Mental Deficiency, New York.

Zarb, G. (1992) 'On the road to Damascus: first steps in changing the relations of disability research production', *Disability, Handicap and Society,* 7, 2, 125-138.

Index

145